Teach Yourself to Write Irresistible Fund-Raising Letters

Conrad Squires

Precept Press, Inc., Chicago

97 96 95 94 93   5 4 3 2 1

Library of Congress Catalog Card Number: 93-083402

International Standard Book Number: 0-944496-38-5

Precept Press, Inc.
160 East Illinois Street
Chicago, Illinois 60611

Printed in the United States of America

*This book is respectfully dedicated to everyone who has ever struggled to find the **best** words to say in a good cause.*

CONTENTS

Contents

CHAPTER

1

Dear Reader

How to Get the Most Out of This Book

Unless you really TRULY hate writing letters, I think or anyway hope you'll enjoy this workbook. It definitely is a WORKbook, by the way, and not a long list of ". . . and then I wrotes." If you use it actively, you should have ten to twelve weeks of extremely useful practice and entertainment ahead of you.

I don't know any other fund-raising book that offers you so many chances to learn by doing. If you use my CopyRater™ and do the exercises in the study units, you are going to be better at writing fundraising letters after you finish this book than you are right now.

I can't teach you writing, though I think working with this book and doing the exercises will help you improve your writing. Its function is to help people who can write learn how to write response-producing fund-raising copy.

There is really no mystery to writing good fund-raising letters. The plain truth is that you already have the knowledge that counts most in writing effective direct mail fund-raising copy. And you come by it naturally. Because it is your understanding of how people think and feel i.e., how you think and feel. If you work from that, and trust it, you'll write strong letters.

The ideas herein come from twenty-two years of writing fund-raising letters and studying response rates and dollars. I have learned in that time that everything you do in your package, or you don't do, has an impact on response.

That's the first and probably the most important idea in this workbook: What you say and how you say it affects the response you get.

Idea number two is this: Any skills I now have I came by the way you get to Carnegie Hall: practice, practice, practice. I can save you some of that work—a lot, actually—because I can point out some mistakes I learned by making them and watching them cost me response.

I should also point out that this book gives you a practice arena that is a safe, private place to learn in.

Here's a final proposition to consider before we go to work: There is much to learn from a fund-raising letter no matter what kind of organization it is written for.

Maybe that's obvious, but I have the feeling that many people in the nonprofit world sit down to write a "hospital" fund-raising letter or a "college" fund-raising letter or a "children's home" letter, et cetera, as if these somehow all require different skills and knowledge. They don't.

The fact is that whoever is mailing it, a letter gets or fails to get response based on who is reading, how compelling the need is, how well written the letter is, and how realistic the "ask" is. Not on what type of institution is sending it out.

This is true because the audience, human beings, remains the same no matter who you are writing for. Your fund-raising letter gets read out there in their world, and it is what they think and feel that determines what kind of response you get.

(Some of the best lessons can be obtained from letters on behalf of places you personally wouldn't give a nickel to—because you can be extremely objective about the techniques in use in those letters.)

So let's remember what we will be studying together in this book is the process of fund-raising letter writing. Take the lessons wherever they come, and don't limit your growth by saying "Well, that's nothing I can use, because it's not my kind of organization."

Using the Workbook

First, make at least twenty copies of the form provided inside the back cover of this book called the CopyRater™. You need these because you will use the CopyRater™ to evaluate the twenty letters presented in the workbook.

Your evaluation is subjective, but the CopyRater™ helps you be systematic about it. It takes you into the heart of the structure of a letter. It's a good predictor of success or failure—a rating that's well below 100 practically guarantees poor response, while a rating of 100 or more guarantees you'll do well (always assuming your letter goes to people who are likely to respond to your cause!). The CopyRater™ highlights the specific weakness or strengths in a letter.

I'm proud of the CopyRater™, because when I was putting it together I wasn't sure it would work at all, but it turned out to work very well. It can help you every time you write or edit a fund-raising letter. That's what many people tell me, and what I observe myself when I use it, which is constantly.

The second chapter, "How to Write a Fund-Raising Letter," reviews the essentials of good letter-writing. It's a highly condensed how-to you may wish to read through a couple of times, then go back to each time you sit down to write a new letter.

You'll find sections on preparing to write, selecting material, writing leads, developing your case, writing your ask, editing your copy, and all the other crucial ingredients.

Next come the twenty Study Units that are the heart of the book. Each Study Unit begins with a fund-raising letter that provides a good example of at least one major factor, either negative or positive, that affects response. The letter is followed by an essay on what's happening (or not happening) in the letter, and that is followed by a suggested exercise you can do to improve the letter. At the back of the book in an Appendix you can find my specific ratings of the letter using the CopyRater™.

First read the letter. Then use the CopyRater™ to evaluate every aspect of it, the lead, the closing, and everything in between. You rate them in a range from Excellent to Unsatisfactory. You select a numerical value for each item in the CopyRater™, and add up your ratings to get an overall value for the letter.

After working the CopyRater™, turn to the CopyRatings section at the back of the workbook and compare your evaluation with mine. There will be some differences, of course, but for the most part I think you will find the evaluations surprisingly similar. Every time I have used the Copy-Rater™ with a group of people in a seminar, the level of agreement has been astonishingly high!

Next read the essay that follows each letter. Key passages in the letter are identified by letter **(A), (B), (C),** et cetera, and are similarly marked in the essay.

Last, do the Suggested Exercises in each Study Unit. These are important because they are aimed at "fixing" apparent weaknesses in the letter example.

Do no more than two Study Units a week, so the lessons have a chance to sink in. Do each exercise in an unhurried way. Treat it as if it were a letter for your own agency. Revise your writing at least two to three times (because revision is necessary to the writing of every good letter).

As you work through the book, the strong direct response techniques and ideas will become more and more obvious to you and the common mistakes will stand out more and more—and those are two huge steps forward when you are creating and then strengthening your own letters.

Once you have thought hard and labored long and rewritten often in the twenty Study Units, some rewards lie just ahead. The final chapters cover such interesting matters as the all-important construction of an interesting, compelling lead paragraph, the crucial decision about how much to ask a prospect or a donor for, how and when you should use enclosures in addition to the letter, and last but not least, how to use personalization effectively, a subject that's been dear to my heart ever since the day I walked into the place the personalized letter was born, Andy Andrews's pioneering company, American Fund Raising Services in Bofton, Maffachufettf . . .

A Shorter Trip

Naturally, I'd like you to spend about a year exclusively on this workbook, doing and revising every exercise, double-checking your ratings, perhaps even taking a day or so off each week to meditate on the abundance of wisdom herein.

But perhaps your time is somewhat limited—or you are a very old hand at this—or you don't actually write, but must evaluate, letters given to you for comment—or any number of other reasons why a long, involved course of study is not possible.

If so, you can still get a great deal from the workbook simply by reading the letters and the essays, and if possible, doing the Copyratings. I would still limit the number of Study Units you do each week to no more than three or four, just to give the ideas in each unit time to "set."

I believe this approach, too, will also yield significant gains for you, though it's not as good, or, to my way of thinking, as much fun, as doing the exercises.

CHAPTER

2

How to Write a Fund-Raising Letter

Who's Your Prospect?

That's me. I'm your prospect.

You got my name from a list of former patients, or alumni, or people in your service area, or I appeared on a list of people who have given to similar causes.

Wherever you located my name, it seemed at least reasonably possible that I might contribute to you, if asked nicely.

But I warn you: when your envelope hits my mailbox, it will be in a competitive environment. It's a jungle in there. Every day!

Your appeal will fight for my time against personal mail, incredibly tempting offers to buy this or that, appeals from other organizations, and the tyranny of the bills.

And a lot of mail that comes to me every day is written by people who make an extremely good living writing the kinds of mailings that tempt people like me to respond. These people are good. They're very good.

And you are up against them.

One thing's for sure: I won't open all my mail. I end up chucking two-thirds of it out before I ever slash the envelope open. I just don't have time for all this stuff!

So your first job is to find a way to get your mailing into the "open me" group of envelopes.

There are lots of ways to do that. You might offer me something free to get me to open you. You might start a good story, something heartwarming or horrifying, something gripping, on the envelope.

You might try a colored envelope—or an odd-sized envelope—to attract my attention.

You might try putting nothing but my name on the outside envelope. I'm always curious about what's inside a plain envelope, so that gives you a real shot. Hey, it might be a chain letter!

You might use two windows, with my name and address in one and something intriguing, such as a free pass to something, showing in the other.

Once I opened an envelope from the National Trust for Historic Preservation because they were offering me a free pass to any of their historic properties. And I ended up contributing!

Well—whatever you did, it worked, because I've opened your envelope and now I'm inside. But you still have a long way to go.

First, is there good follow-through between what you did on the outside envelope and the first thing I'll see inside?

Since whatever you put on the outside is why I opened your envelope, there certainly should be immediate follow-through. If you offered a premium, describe it now. If you started a story, continue it now.

Don't even wait for "Dear Friend" to make its appearance! Get on!

Second, since it's a fund-raising letter, have you made it extremely easy for me to see exactly what you want my money for?

Have you made it clear how much you want? Answer "no" to either question, and you'll probably lose me.

Let's say I have opened three appeals, one of which is yours, and though I'd like to, I can't send money to all three.

Which one will I respond to? The one that interests me the most and moves me the most.

Alas, it probably won't be the agency that needs my help the most, or the agency that has the best, most efficient organization. It will be the one that sent me the best letter.

That's because I'm not really responding to your organization, I'm responding to your appeal.

Your appeal can be angry, intense, emotional, urgent, storytelling, dramatic, quiet. It can be bricks and mortar, the feeding of children, the saving of souls.

6

Whatever it is, if you want me as a donor, make me feel the warmth of other people's lives, the reality of other people's needs.

Make me feel that in giving I will be acting in a noble and generous way. Make me feel no matter how small my gift is, it counts.

(Don't, don't, don't let me feel that once I send my gift I won't hear from you again!—Don't say, for instance, that we're saving money for the cause by not sending me a thank you letter!)

Listen, don't get discouraged. There really is a chance, a good chance, that I will contribute to you. All you have to do is take your time, write a good, honest, specific, strong letter.

Persuade me. I actually want to help. Because every time I do, it makes me feel good about myself.

Who's Your Donor?

That's me. I used to be your prospect, but I'm your donor now.

I told you I might help! Back in those days I was a prospect, a nameless one. But you found me among hundreds of people.

You made me feel you were meeting a real need.

You made me feel you needed me—me personally.

I thought, because of what you said, "That IS worth supporting!" Though I didn't put it this way consciously, I was thinking, "This will make the world a little better."

You made me feel that a contribution to your cause would not be swallowed up, digested and forgotten—that our contacts would be frequent and warm.

And once I had sent my donation, I wasn't disposed to doubt you. In fact, based on what you said in your letter, I believe strongly in what your organization stands for.

But I certainly do want you to thank me, the sooner the better, the friendlier the better.

And after the thank you, I really do not want you to wait a year or even six months before contacting me again. If you wait that long, I will know you really didn't want anything to do with me, you just want to tap me for money once a year.

Listen, I have a brother-in-law for that! And he comes twice a year! Sometimes more!

I'd like to hear from you regularly. If you have a newsletter, I'd like to get that and anything else you have that tells me what the organization is doing.

What's more, if there are ways I can help you in addition to sending money, I'd like to know. The more you ask me to do, the more I actually do, the closer I feel to the organization.

For heaven's sakes, don't be cold and official when you write to me. I don't want to be outside, supporting you, I want to be inside, participating in what you do!

These things are important if you want to keep me.

I've been around the block a few times, you know. I've given to other causes and been disappointed. Oh sure, we started off well, but then they'd seem to change their tune with each new letter.

Sometimes it was as if they never heard of me—me, their donor! But I'm hoping that won't be true this time.

We'll see.

The Path to Better Letters Begins Here: The Short Course

You can improve response to your next letter by making it simpler, both visually and verbally, which means shorter lines, larger type, no board lists, elaborate, distracting design and above all, fewer ideas.

Concentrate on the main task, which is to "Raise the money!"

Let me tell you something I have seen NO exceptions to in 22 years of writing direct mail fund-raising letters—the letters that work hardest to get the money get the most money.

Make sure each paragraph "grows" right out of the preceding one, i.e., carries on and extends the topic in the preceding one. That makes easy, smooth reading. Readers like that.

And let there be no digressions—none. Keep your eye on your objective.

Make your letter warmer. Choose a friend, a relative, and write to him or her. Make it more specific. Be as specific as you possibly can about what the money is needed for and how much you are asking for.

Make it more reader-focused. Give the reader 100% of the credit in advance for whatever you want to accomplish. You take 0.

Then when you edit your letter—a couple of days after you write it—watch for these danger signals of low response: slow start; position paper; we-oriented.

The Long Course

We began to define donors and prospects above. Now let's go a little further. A donor is somebody who believes in what you are doing and believes she is doing it with you. He is to be written to and treated as an insider—really, not tactically.

A prospect is somebody who knows little or nothing about your organization and cares less. He is not looking forward to sending you money and she is pretty sure you will disappear as soon as she does send you money. And you have to overcome all that, if you can, in your copy.

What's Your Copy Purpose?

Write down what the package or packages of the campaign are supposed to achieve. Not the dollar goals, just a line or two:

This letter to people who have given before is to ask them to renew this year and to send a larger gift to help meet the increased need for. . . .

This letter to people who know the institution but have not given before is to ask them each to give a small, easily given gift and thereby get them into the donor base, with upgrading to follow in later campaigns. . . .

This letter is to people who have not given during the past two campaigns. It tells them they have been seriously missed and offers a way they can rejoin easily. . . .

And so on. The Copy Purpose must contain two elements—the relationship you have with the person who will read the letter, and the specific kind of request you will make, based on that relationship.

This Copy Purpose becomes the writer's primary guideline.

Three more things must be nailed down for the writer—the need or needs that is/are the subject of the campaign—the benefits that will come to donors as a result of participation—and the production data, if any, that is developed on the package before the writer begins.

(There probably should be some leeway on this last point, which boils down to, will the letter be computer- or laser-printed or printed offset, how many pages, what size stationery, any special inserts, et cetera.)

We'll talk more about these things later—the point here is that if these things have been worked out in in advance, the writer should know what they are before he or she begins.

Here's Rule Number One

The writer and his editor (there should definitely be an editor) now have an excellent written series of checkpoints to evaluate the copy with. And one primary rule to follow, herewith: anything in a letter that does not clearly make a contribution to the Copy Purpose must go.

Pre-Writing

Now the writer has to go to work. He must gather data, organize it, outline it. If it is not preassigned, he must select *one* activity of the agency that will serve as an example of all the rest—almost always, this should be the one that would have the most emotional impact on prospective donors.

He must link the listed benefits to his "ask." Often it's effective to give the benefits the lion's share of the space in a letter.

He should talk to people in the organization. If he's from outside, he has to get a sense of the energy of the organization; if he's from inside he has to draw back from the mundane day-to-day life and think about what the organization is *there to do.*

Theme

To achieve the Copy Purpose, which always boils down to—Raise Money—a direct mail letter also has to be about something else. It must be about people. And concrete, understandable needs. Not a laundry list that is so long it conveys no feeling to the reader. Clear, obvious, simple human needs.

Try hard to make people feel the warmth of other lives through your letters. Not because that's what makes good writing, but because that makes good reading. And therefore gets response.

Think about what people are interested in as you choose your themes. Curing cancer, feeding the hungry, saving children, offering life-saving care, helping people rehabilitate themselves, providing scholarship help— you can practically put these things in rank order as to how well people will respond, and you must be thinking about such things when you choose your themes.

Using Your Budget

Look at your budget and pull out the things that represent the most direct, personal help to people. Use them to represent your services and use them, whenever you possibly can, with story illustrations. Be a sponge for human interest stories and count on the fact that the stories that will move you will move your donors, too.

How Long Should Your Letter Be?

If it's really a telegram or a simulated telegram, the shorter it is, the better it appears to pull.

If it's a letter, all I can tell you is that I've had strong 28-line letters and strong 6-page letters. Quien sabe? Just don't write longer than you have to.

I will say this—if I had to stake my whole professional future, our house, the car, and my Japanese guitar on just one letter, it would be a long letter.

I like Jerry Huntsinger's story about being a vacuum cleaner salesman. If he couldn't get in the door he had no sale, if he could only get a few minutes he had no sale, but if he could get a half hour or more, he had a sale.

But keep your sentences short, paragraphs short, your content maximum, your verbosity minimum. And if you've written a long letter, make sure it is interesting! You can probably live with the response from a short, dull letter, but a long dull one is a disaster!

Your Lead

A good lead needs to be interesting and if possible fast reading. It starts your case-for-the-gift and its one purpose is to get your reader to decide to read on.

Well, how do you do that? Start by thinking about the reader. The great direct mailman Robert Collier wrote that everyone has a constant mental conversation with himself, and the subject is "I"—why can't I make more money, more friends, get a promotion, how'd I do yesterday, how will I do today, why won't my lawn grow . . .

Collier said, "In your lead you must find a way to chime in with that conversation." For instance:

> "I don't think the world really knows just how generous you are, but we certainly do, Mr. Smith . . ."

> "You've proven that you are somebody who really cares what happens to children, Mr. Smith . . ."

> "Your amazing kindness can change the world for Meta Singh and his family, Mr. Smith . . ."

> "Your gift of $000 last October helped put the
> finishing touches on the rectory, dear friend!"

> "You are cordially invited to join a . . ." (Al-
> ways a good lead, because it goes right to peo-
> ple's strong associative desires.)

Please take it as revealed truth that the reader is very interested in anything you have to say about him. The more space you spend writing about the reader, the better response you're likely to get.

Either the lead chimes in with the mental conversation the reader is already having as the above examples do, or it offers something else so interesting it distracts the reader, e.g., "I have important news about a breakthrough in the fight against cancer."

A natural, personal lead is usually best. I wrote for an Indian mission school some years ago and my typical lead was something like this,

> "Boy is it ever cold up here in North Dakota
> right now, Mr. Smith!"

Today, thanks to the magic of computers and lasers, I would probably write, "You might find it hard to believe down there in Tampa how horrendously cold it is up here in North Dakota right now, Mr. Smith!"

Story-telling leads are wonderful when the stories are not forced:

> "New York City isn't the big unfriendly place
> Martha Chiang thought it was when she first
> arrived."

Watch out for warm-up in your leads. Warmup is is what you write while you're working up your nerve to start making your real case.

> "You may be wondering why the Salvation
> Army is writing to you at this time." (He isn't)

> "The basic purpose of Keep America Beautiful
> is to show Americans there is a better way to
> keep America beautiful." (Warm-up!)

Watch out for the deadly assumption that your agency's concerns are more important than the reader's concerns. They are—to you. Not to him.

One I recently read went something like this:

> "Let's talk about priorities. Yours and ours.
> First ours."

> "Pause and take a breather . . . and while you are relaxing, please consider my appeal for your help."

> "The most important thing in the world is a child. Your child. Your neighbor's child. Any child. A child is the hope of the future."

> "Hoka! Hokahe! shouted Little Turtle as he led the charge."

(Actually, I have always suspected that's a good lead. I just don't remember what it was for!)

Want to get a good response? Write a serious lead. Here are two great ones, classics:

> "I am writing to you today to ask for your help in supporting our craft kit program to distribute arts and crafts materials to sick and seriously wounded veterans in military and VA hospitals throughout the United States."

> "I would like to ask you to join me in forming a new, independent non-partisan organization to help in rebuilding this nation. It will be known as Common Cause. It will not be a third party but a third force in American life, deriving its strength from a common desire to solve the nation's problems and revitalize its institutions of government."

These leads are long, but they are long because they take themselves and their mission very seriously. And both got great results.

The Middle Development

In the lead paragraph you started your case. Now any number of things can happen but one thing *must* happen.

The case must continue to be developed, whether it is developing inside a story you are telling or through the expanded description of a problem you started in the lead or whatever else you started with.

I think this is a real danger point for any letter-writer. It is the moment, if you haven't done it before, to create an outline of the development of your case, and then stick to it. Digressions are so easy! Let me give you an example:

> "I am writing to ask you to help put the roof back on the church, which you probably remember left us during the recent cyclone."
>
> "The Board of Deacons has set a number of priorities for various reconstruction projects this year, and established prudent guidelines for the management of all the tasks included."
>
> "I know this point will be particularly important to you as you consider how much you can give to put a new roof on the church."

How easy! How dangerous! Whatever your case is, outline it, and stick to it!

And show how the problem can be solved—turns out it can usually be solved with money.

The Ask

Say you eliminated your warmup and got off a lead that was interesting, reader-oriented, and made a strong start for your case.

Say in your next paragraph or two or three you showed exactly how crucial your need is, and how important the reader's help will be.

Now we have arrived at the part of the letter every reader knows is coming, and possibly dreading.

Put it the wrong way, suggest something out of the question, and you're out of the ballgame.

The question is . . .? (how much?)

How do You Say How Much?

Would you say, "We need a million five so anything you send will be welcome"?

Would you say, "We need a million five so if everybody sends $10 we're home free"?

Would you say, "We need so much money this year I want you to send three times as much as you ever sent before?" (sometimes)

Would you say, "You can see how serious the children's needs are and up here just a little money buys a lot. If you can manage to send a gift of

$10, $15 or even more, it can buy a coat to keep the chill North Wind off a child's back''?

Would you say, ''This need is so compelling that if you usually send $15, won't you please try to send $20 or more—and if $25 is your normal giving level, won't you stretch to a gift of $30, $40 or even more?''

Would you say, ''This remarkable life-saving instrument costs about $25,000. For this reason we're hoping that you'll take five or even ten 'shares' of the purchase at $25 per share?''

Yup. That's a very strong way to put your ''ask.''

Andy Andrews of American Fund Raising Services, who may have forgotten more about direct mail than I've learned, once wrote a really nonsensical ask.

He said (more or less) ''We're celebrating our 25th birthday this year. Won't you help celebrate by putting a '25' in your gift and sending $15.25, $25.25, $50.25 or even more?'' Nonsense, right? It worked like crazy!

Donors

When you're writing to donors, in my opinion, your best bet is to find a way to ask them for a little more than they as individuals gave last time. Lots of ways to do that.

With donors, the higher you go the softer the upgrade and the more polite your ask. You lose one $500 donor and you have lost 20 $25 donors, so renewal, year in and year out, is much more important than upgrading at the higher level.

Prospects

When you're mailing to prospects, you have, in my opinion, two options.

You can ask for a small, easily given gift:

> ''Won't you send just $15, knowing children's lives are on the line?''

Why is that good? Because it brings the maximum number of people into your donor file. And it yields the most dollars, too. Second alternative—''This is so important, some people have sent contributions of $500, $1,000 and even more, others are sending $15, $20, $30, $50, $100 and more.''

Principle—it hits each reader at his or her own normal of giving and draws the occasional large gift that was just lying there waiting for somebody to ask for it.

Rule Number Two

The more time you spend in your letter talking about the specific gift you want the reader to send, the more response you will be apt to get. Why? Because your letter is about the donor's money. There is nothing in your package that will have as big an impact as a good piece of ''ask'' thinking.

The Post-Script

I agree with everybody else. Do write one. It sticks out all by itself and just has to be a high readership point in your letter.

Use it to resell your proposition:

> "Remember, the goal you and I share is to control cancer in OUR lifetimes."

Use it to add a note of urgency as in this famous example:

> "We have just 30 days to pay off the mortgage on Liberty Mountain."

(That sounds a little like a Disney movie.)

Use it to make an offer of recognition:

> "It surely would be fine to see the name of Mr. David A. Smith among the S's on our Bronze Donor Honor Roll."

(Or, in one memorable campaign for an aquarium ''. . . in our Golden Log Book.'')

Recognition is a POWERFUL incentive. Use it every chance you get, in every way you can think of.

The Add-on

When you finish your P.S. you really should stop writing and get ready to battle to keep other people from adding in ideas—unless, of course, you forgot something you needed.

The add-on is the curse of direct mail fund-raising. You write a tight letter and someone reads and says, "This is great, but shouldn't we mention such-and-such?" Ditto the next person, the next, the next. The last person reads it and says, "This is okay, but why is it so long?"

Add-ons cut into response. They lose readers and cost you money.

Use of Supporting Materials

I think you get a "yes" or "no" decision with your letter and a final "how-much" decision when the person has your reply slip in one hand and checkbook in the other.

Don't mail a routine information folder. It's wasted money. I've seen a letter/folder combination tested three times against the same letter all by itself—nice-looking folders, well-written (by me)—and each time the presence of the folder appeared to depress response.

There are times when you have to have a folder, however, and here they are: When you need to present your story visually as well as verbally—when you want to sell/sell/sell the benefits—when you need to add a subject that's not in the letter but is necessary—when you want to add a newspaper clipping or other special enclosure—when you are including a front-end premium.

The Reply Slip

First, I think you should use a slip and a reply envelope rather than a deep-flap wallet reply envelope. It's cheaper. You can tailor it to your particular appeal.

The reply slip is a straight re-sell of the case for a gift in your letter. "Help feed the hungry," "Help purchase the scanner," "Arthritis hurts. Help us stop the pain." Make it self-standing—enough information so that if you left your letter out you'd still get some response.

Make the slip a bright color. Make it stand out. Identify it clearly as the reply slip. Say it MUST come with the gift. Keep it brisk and fairly businesslike and simple to fill out.

Don't offer your donor or prospect a sermon on the reply slip: "Yes, I agree the plight of American womanhood is a profoundly important cause and I fully support the efforts of the whatever to accomplish these five critical goals in. . . ." Keep it simple.

Membership card and benefits, upgrade gift circled, "Can you send this?", premium offer, special recognition offer . . .

Editing

After you write, wait a couple of days before editing it. Make yourself wait!

Is it easy to read? Is it interesting? Is the request clear? Is it appropriate to the people on the list? Does it square with the Copy Purpose? Is it simple, believable, direct? Will it draw an emotional response from the reader? Is it only as long as it has to be?

If you find for the copywriter in these matters, your letter's in pretty good shape.

Preachy

Try, try, try to avoid the sense that people owe you the support you know your cause merits.

I once wrote for an organization trying to get emergency help into Cambodia in the days when the Khmer Rouge were running things and interdicting all the trails.

I wanted to say to my American neighbors, "Look, you and I have much more than we need and these people have nothing. That's wrong! We were put on this earth to share, so come on, let's share!"

That's true, I guess, but it wouldn't have worked. People go to be preached at in church and not very many, if any, other places.

In the end, all I did was say what the organization was doing, exactly, and how the donor could help. At the end, I added, "The Bible says there is a purpose for every thing under the heavens. This is a time to plant."

Since the appeal was for seeds, plows, hoes and oxen, I thought I could give myself a little leeway in this area.

Just give a prospect a chance to make somebody's life better, to be part of a world in which people help each other. That's all you really need to do.

18

Painting a Picture

If you want to win good response you need to find a way to make your appeal come to life in a reader's head. Use word pictures to do this—make everything you're talking about as real and as vivid as you can.

And create a clear human need before you begin talking about financial need.

Formula-Busting

We have formulas to work from, but we always find ourselves in fund-raising situations where the formulas and guidelines don't quite apply. Then we have to think, improvise, and break ground. And you know what? People seem to respond better!

We're on the sea of human behavior. It's not well charted. It's the blessing and curse of our trade that this particular seascape is always the same and always new. I don't think this seascape ever will be mapped. I don't think the "final analysis," the "total donor strategy" will ever be written or programmed.

The heart, which has a very nice sense of self-preservation, is probably always going to hide its inmost reasons from us.

A Confession

I recently spent two days filing fund-raising letters I had written. Huge piles of them. It was a chastening experience.

Most of the first day I was down in the dumps. I kept seeing letters that were routine, letters that made me feel I should have worked harder to be interesting, letters that had a good lead and a weak case, letters that represented times I let clients talk me into themes that in my heart I already knew would not fly when they reached the donors . . .

Making it worse is that I have kept hundreds of good letters from great mailers like Covenant House, Father Flanagan's, the Nature Conservancy and so many others—letters written by Jerry Huntsinger, Art Cone, Andy Andrews and many other writers who shine brightly in the mail fund-raising firmament.

Thinking about all those good letters and letter writers left me even more depressed—bear in mind, I only save what I like. It started to look to me as if the entire direct mail world were writing better letters than I was!

19

On the second day, though, I began getting into letters that made me feel better. Letters with feeling, letters with good stories, letters with riveting leads, letters that worked hard to keep a reader interested, letters that took chances, letters that presented big, daring ideas, clever "ask" paragraphs that produced some memorably big gifts—and some letters I just plain am proud of for no one particular reason.

Honest efforts, every one.

It seemed to me that the main difference between the letters I liked and the ones I didn't like was this: in the ones I like I had followed my natural instincts as a writer, and used all that I have learned as a fund-raiser, rather than executing formulas put forward by other people or copying letters I'd done in the past that fit the current situation "well enough."

To write the letters that I liked, I had gone into my head and heart, not my swipe file.

Well, what's the moral? For the most part, the letters I liked the best also turned out to pull the best. You might want to think about that when you sit down to write your next letter. Work for quality, for sincerity, to express your feelings as well as you can—and donors will understand and will respond.

CHAPTER

3

The Study Units

STUDY UNIT

1

Why an informal writing style is a great tool

(Sample: a college fund raising letter)

TO: All parents of Current and Former Students

FROM: Mrs. Grace M. Smith, mother of Mary Smith

SUBJECT: Annual Appeal for 1984

My daughter Mary has just completed her junior year at Auburndale College. Before moving into the Upper College as a Junior, Mary, like all Auburndale students, had to successfully complete Moderation, a singular feature of the College's rigorous educational program. At Moderation, each student assesses academic accomplishment, reviews strengths and weaknesses, and explores plans for the final two years at Auburndale in a two- or-three hour session with a panel of three faculty members—all in terms of his or her intellectual and/or artistic goals. **(A)**

Moderation is only one aspect of Auburndale's system of evaluating the needs and encouraging the intellectual growth of its students: there are special freshman advisers to help entering students make the most of that critically important year, and the Freshman Seminars are designed to give first-year students a solid common background from which to pursue their individual interests in the following three years; sophomore-year programs lead to the Moderation described above; a junior conference—with widely different manifestations in each of the College's four academic divisions—encourages the upper class student to investigate in detail a subject of particular interest in his or her major field; and, finally, the Senior Project, accomplished with close faculty supervision, is a major piece of creative, critical, or analytical work, comparable in intensity and scope to the Master's thesis at other institutions, and is the culmination of the student's tenure at Auburndale. **(B)**

Auburndale is truly exceptional, not only in its exacting academic programs, not only in its nurturing of the special talents and abilities of each individual student, but also in this system of intellectual and creative safeguards and check-points, carefully designed to guarantee that Auburndale students develop realistic and worthwhile goals for their lives as well as the capacity to achieve them.

I am convinced that my daughter's experience at Auburndale could not be equalled at any other educational institution. I am also certain that when Mary goes to law school in the Fall of 1985, she will be fully equipped to deal with whatever she encounters there. Even more important, I know that Auburndale is preparing Mary to be a responsible, creative, and contributing member of our complex and everchanging society.

That is why I am supporting the Auburndale College Fund. **(C)** Won't you join me and the many other parents of current and former Auburndale students who make annual gifts to the Fund to insure that Auburndale's extraordinary educational programs continue to flourish?

Your check of $10, $50, $500 dollars—more if your circumstances permit—will directly bene- fit Auburndale students, now and in years to come. **(D)**

Suggested Study Procedure

1. Read the letter straight through at your normal reading pace. Ask yourself, "Good, bad, or somewhere in between?"
2. Re-read the letter slowly.
3. Use the CopyRater™ to evaluate the letter in detail. Add your score. Then note the most important strengths and weaknesses.
4. Compare your ratings with the author's at the back of the workbook.
5. Read the essay at the end of this Study Unit.
6. Write the suggested Exercise material.
7. Review all the work, then add the most important idea(s) to your own developing personal list of letter-writing guidelines.

Suggested Exercises

1. Short of rewriting the entire letter, please correct the biggest single weakness you find in this letter.
2. Be the parent of Mary Smith and address this letter to a parent of another Auburndale student. What would be natural to say? Write just two or three paragraphs—and keep your main objective in mind.
3. Write a good "ask" paragraph based on applicable material in the "How to" chapter at the back—again, in parent-to-parent context.

Comments About This Letter

When an appeal is in real trouble, the problems aren't just in the copy. In this case, an immediate conceptual difficulty is the manner of address above the letter body.

The best-pulling fund-raising letters usually have the sound and feel of one friendly person writing to another. Would you choose a memo format to convey friendship and warmth?

If you were a parent of a college student writing to a parent of another college student, would you choose a memo format?

If you wanted your letter to be read as a personal communication, would you say "TO: All parents of Current and Former Auburndale Students?"

The memo format is an institution's major means of distributing uniform information widely, president to students, dean to faculty, et al.

It would be extremely hard to create a form less likely to evoke the emotional spark that must be present in good fund-raising letters.

Starting Off Right: Friend to Friend

What would you do to make this an effective communication? I think you must try to establish a bond between the two parents at once:

```
Mr. and Mrs. Arthur Mann
22 Lake Avenue
Boston, MA 02166
```

"Dear Parents of an Auburndale Student:"

"I hope your youngster's experiences at Auburndale have been as positive as our daughter Mary's have been. We've been sending extra support for Auburndale's programs and hope you'll join us."

That's a friend writing to a potential friend. The two parents or two sets of parents do have a bond—several years of shared experiences. That really is something to build on.

To build rapport, the logical raw materials are what the kids have told the parents about the college—what Mary has told Susan, what the other child told his or her parents.

Does that happen in this letter?

This paragraph might have been lifted intact out of the admissions materials—in fact, I bet it was. But why tell another parent what "moderation" is? They already know.

Tone and Length

Tone is important in a direct mail letter. Let's define "tone" as being, quite simply, what you "sound like" in print, your personal style, which derives from the way you organize your thoughts in writing, from your choices of words, from your formality or lack of same, all combining to give the reader an impression of the writer.

(A) Does this paragraph, do any of the paragraphs, remotely resemble the tone of a real letter from one parent of a college student writing informally to another? Of course it doesn't! The tone of this letter is that of a college catalogue, which is probably where most of it came from.

As you can see, length is central to the creation of a tone—length of words, length of sentences, length of paragraphs. In this letter, everything is too long!

After creating many mailings and watching people respond, I have come to feel that sheer reading speed (by which I don't mean brevity but the easy, swift flow of words and ideas from one paragraph to the next) is an extremely important indicator of fund-raising success.

The basic ways to create a letter that can be swiftly read are: 1) use the shortest, clearest words that say exactly what you mean; 2) limit yourself strictly to one clearly stated idea per paragraph; 3) make the idea in the next paragraph flow directly and easily out of the idea in the preceding one.

Here's an example of limiting the ideas to one per paragraph, making each idea flow out of the preceding paragraph, and keeping the words simple.

> "I need your immediate financial help to re-
> place the roof on the parish hall."
> "We can't reopen Sunday School until we re-
> place that roof."
> "And if we're not providing Sunday School for
> our kids, we're not teaching them to love God."
> "So please help right away! Send the biggest
> gift you can manage to replace the roof on the
> parish hall!"

(B) In fairly stark contrast, I count 108 words in this one-sentence paragraph, which I defy you to read for sense. Some experts feel that when a sentence exceeds eight words, dropoff in readership begins. One hundred words too late!

The paragraph is a masterpiece of college catalogue style, encapsulating four years of a young person's life inside a capital letter, a period, one colon, three semicolons, nine commas, two double dashes and several possessives. (Any resemblance to living speech is coincidental.)

Where's the Reader? Where's the Ask?

We're now twenty-one long lines of hard reading into the appeal. There has been no mention of the reader (who ought to be the main subject of any fund-raising appeal, i.e., How you can personally help bring an end to the destruction of cancer).

Money has not been mentioned either.

(C) The entire "ask" is contained in this paragraph. It centers on insuring "That Auburndale's extraordinary educational programs continue to flourish."

That may be enough of a reason to give. But wouldn't something specific, such as the need to improve student housing, do better, especially if developed as a theme throughout the letter?

The prospect is asked to support the institution, the whole institution, and nothing but the institution. Not the services, not any specific programs, not student aid, which is a strong theme for alumni (not sure about parents). I believe institutional vanity, frequently in evidence here, is one of the deadliest of all Copy Sins.

What came across to me is that I should support them because they merit support. But most donors, in my view, send money because they feel what's happening merits support, and that's not the same thing.

Make Your Gift Range Realistic

(D) The gift ranging here, "$10, $50, $500 is too broad to be a collection of real choices for a prospect. This is an extremely common mistake.

Gift ranging is done because response is higher when people know what is expected of them, but you can't accomplish this when the amounts are as spread out as they are here.

Here's a better approach, using much the same language:

"Your tax-deductible check in any amount, whether it is $10, $15, $20, or even $50, $100 or more, will directly benefit Auburndale students . . ."

Keeping the first three amounts close together has a positive impact on response percentage and on bringing in a larger average gift. In a very interesting test last year, I saw a $10, $12, $14 suggested gift range produce much more income than a $10, $15, $20 suggested range.

In Conclusion

What was the copy purpose of this letter? It was or should have been to persuade a parent to send a gift. But you don't reach the copy purpose until the final paragraph. This means the writer was not at all focused on the task, and it also means that the letter failed to pull well.

The case for a gift should have begun in the first paragraph. It should have been linked to Mary's real experiences, none of which appear in this letter. That wouldn't have been hard to do:

"My daughter Mary was really nervous as her
Moderation got near—was your child nervous,
too?"

The case should have been pegged to the pride parents feel as their children progress and the growing affection parents feel for a college in which their children are having a success. Those are the emotional motivators for a gift from a parent.

The paragraphs should be shorter. (Actually, if I liked hunting and that second paragraph were a bighorn sheep trophy I would certainly hang it in my den if I had a den. It is the longest single sentence I have ever seen in a fund-raising appeal.)

STUDY UNIT

2

Put your reader's interests first

(Sample: letter to prospects from Planned Parenthood)

(A) Dear David:

It is all a question of priorities—yours and ours. **(B)** First ours . . .

(C) Very simply, Planned Parenthood is one of the most important causes in the world. Overpopulation is at the root of most of the major problems of our time: poverty, hunger and malnutrition, neglect and child abuse. The unwanted child is a tragic figure in our country as well as in Bombay. Yet our style, as a voluntary family planning agency, is to emphasize individual choice, human dignity and freedom. As government funds are cut (32% this year), individual donations must increase.

(D) Families are strongest when they are planned. Planned Parenthood of North Central Auburndale's primary purpose is to help people have the children they want, if any, when they want them. We believe that the birthright of every child is a loving home, a decent life, and a future of hope. We further believe that unless people have the ability to plan their families, they will have little control over other aspects of their lives.

(E) There is enormous unmet need in Auburndale. Last year only 28.5% of the number of women estimated to be in need of low-cost care were served. Let me explain how our programs begin to meet this need.

PPNCA is a private, non-profit agency providing comprehensive family planning services in a four-county area in (our area). With its administrative offices in (city), PPNCA operates clinics in (various cities). Services provided in each clinic include:

(F) (a 9-line list of services appeared here)

(G) Through resource loans and direct presentations, the community education department of PPNCA provides area schools, social agencies, churches and community groups with comprehensive information in the area of sex education and family life.

PPNCA has been providing services in this area for more than 15 years. In each of the counties served, PPNCA is the only provider of low-cost family planning services designed specifically to meet the needs of women and families who ordinarily have difficulty obtaining or affording private medical care.

To achieve its purpose, PPNCA works in two major ways. First, we provide family planning services to help people understand the implications and consequences of childbearing; to help them, if necessary, with the decision-making process; and to help them carry out their decisions through informed use of high-quality family planning services. Second, we attempt to influence the social/political environment so that support for the availability of family planning information and services continues to grow in our communities. PPNCA is proud that last year we served 7,114 patients. Nearly half (3,496) were new patients, the highest amount ever.

Your donation is extremely important to keep up with this increase in services.

Now, about your priorities. As you are be-
sieged with requests for money in 1982, think:
with your support, PPNCA will continue to
strengthen family life in our community.

Sincerely,

Name
Position

P.S. I urge you to read the enclosed copy of a
mother's cry for help. Your donation sent today
will help make every child a wanted child.

Suggested Study Procedure

1. Read the letter straight through at your normal reading pace. Ask yourself, "Good, bad, or somewhere in between?"
2. Re-read the letter slowly.
3. Use the CopyRater™ to evaluate the letter in detail. Add your score. Then note the most important strengths and weaknesses.
4. Compare your ratings with the author's at the back of the workbook.
5. Read the essay at the end of this Study Unit.
6. Write the suggested Exercise material.
7. Review all the work, then add the most important idea(s) to your own developing personal list of letter-writing guidelines.

Exercises

1. Short of rewriting the entire letter, please correct the biggest single weakness you find in this letter.
2. Find the most important thing Planned Parenthood does, as stated in the letter, and write a lead paragraph of no more than four lines based on the need to support that service.
3. Take Paragraph Two and alter everything in it so that the items are the reader's personal concerns, not the organization's concerns.

Comments About This Letter

Here's a useful point to remember when writing your own letters: the person you should be writing to is someone who shares your sense of the worth of what you are doing, who thinks much as you do. No fund-raising letter ever wins an argument.

You are or should be focusing on people who agree with you and who will contribute if they can, if asked properly. People who disagree with you will not contribute no matter what you say, so don't aim your letters at the objectors.

Because the prospect is already in sympathy with what you're doing, your letter should not so much be about your organization as about what the prospect can do to strengthen your mutual cause.

That's a good starting point. In its original form, this letter had 58 lines. Of these, 49 were devoted to a detailed explanation of what the organization's goals are and how it accomplishes them.

Just nine lines (give or take) were about you, the reader. But were they really? Read the you lines carefully.

I feel it is more of a position paper than a letter. As such, I would say it's pretty good. But position papers are written for the purpose of stating or clarifying your position on something, not for raising money. A position paper doesn't invite, or get, much response.

(A) The letter had a full inside address (not shown) and the salutation you see. It was expensive to produce, or would have been in large quantities. But the personalization is not functional, that is, it doesn't suggest that the reader has any sort of special relationship with the agency, either as a donor or an interested prospect.

If it was mailed to donors, it missed the one most crucial point—the donor's special inside status. It costs you when you don't recognize that status in letters to donors. I think the donor's status is the true primary subject of any donor letter and it is the fact of prior support that makes him most likely to support you now.

But assume this isn't a donor letter. If not, I think the salutation is a little off track. In a fund-raising letter, I'm put off by first-name informality from an organization I've had no association with.

A Communication "Basic"

(B) The lead paragraph illustrates the basic problem in the letter. Whose priorities are by far more important to the reader? So why on earth would you say, First ours?''

Robert Collier, a great direct mailer, once wrote that every person is constantly holding a mental conversation with himself. The subject of this conversation with himself—his hopes, his dreams, his unmet needs, his successes, what others think of him, his worries.

To be heard in the din of that mental conversation, you must be able to chime in with the thoughts he is having, and to show him that you too have his best interests uppermost in your mind. Then he will read what you have to say.

What an insight Collier provides! Surely this is the essence of all serious attempts to communicate with other people. If you wish someone to listen, you must chime in with the other person's mental world, a world of "self." You cannot, as this letter does, start from the assumption that your concerns are of greater importance than your reader's concerns.

I believe the error in this first paragraph was probably fatal to the appeal. Persons who already have strong commitments to the organization will probably respond, but those less strongly committed, and those who favor the organization but have no commitment to it, will not have responded.

The latter groups are the ones who make or break any direct mail appeal, donor or prospect—the ones who will give if you really reach them with what you said and the way you said it. In this case, I think they stopped reading long before the end.

(C) A paragraph should have just one topic, maximum. This one has three topics, two too many. They are: overpopulation as a world problem—what the agency is like—government cuts and the need for more donations. Each of these should have been developed in a separate paragraph.

I appreciate the importance of solving the population problem, but it seems inappropriate for a regional family planning agency. Wouldn't the reader be more interested in the specific problems of his or her region?

Stories, Not Statistics

Also, instead of reciting ideas and statistics, wouldn't it be more effective to dramatize this (or any other) appeal with the stories of real people? This agency, like all human service agencies, receives contributions from people who want to help other people. So why not illustrate that with stories?

(D) The next paragraph expresses the agency's philosophy. It is better to show than tell, and I think these concepts should be illustrated, not stated.

(E) Now we come to an unmet need. But I can't see exactly what the need is, just as I don't know exactly what is meant by "were served." I think the following paragraph, "PPNCA is . . ." doesn't really show how the agency meets the unmet need. It says what has been done for the

28.5%. Well, it doesn't actually do that either, it describes the services and organization of the agency.

I believe lack of clarity and long paragraphs that express many ideas and are not tightly tied to the preceding paragraph (see COMMENTS, Study Unit 1) reduce readership. Readers, it must be said, are not going to put themselves out for you. They won't make a big effort to read something that's hard going.

Flow is a special problem in this letter. I have read it perhaps more times than most people would read a fund-raising letter and at this moment I would hate to have to take a test on what's in it. That's not good. People have to get what you mean, first time.

(F) Lists are deadly. They stop the flow of a letter totally. Avoid them at all costs. If you have to have a list, put it in a separate enclosure, not in the middle of your case for a gift.

(G) The next paragraphs, down to "Your donation . . ." continue the agency's self-description. They do not refer to the need for financial support. Of 54 lines of body copy to that point, only one mentioned a need for donations.

The word "you" is used just once. I don't know how much to belabor this point, which comes up again and again, but the emphasis in the letter is exactly the wrong way around. The proper subject of a fund-raising letter is not the organization but the need for money, and there should be many "you's."

What's wrong, I think, is that the people who work for the agency feel, reasonably, that people support it on the basis of its worth as an agency.

To me that's a mistake. I believe people respond not to an institution but to a need, to its urgency, to its natural priority among their personal concerns, to the way it makes them feel to be doing something about that particular need.

And they respond to the degree to which the institution makes them feel their personal response is important, that the response stamps them as people who care, who are responsible (no pun intended).

So you go to the largest expression of your cause.

If you are raising money for a school, you talk about the children who are our future. If you are raising money for a hospital, you talk about how helping to build a new operating suite will improve the surgical procedures for thousands of patients. And so on.

Seeing Yourself as Others See You

It is difficult to be inside an institution and sense how what you do feels to people outside. But in writing your letters you need to get outside mentally, and look at the institution from the donor's point of view—not what it is but what it's for.

And then of course you have to be ready to defend the copy you have based on that point of view, because everyone you will show it to inside the institution has the same problem you do. I wrote a letter that was successful for a big hospital. After it had mailed for several years and was doing well, I went to lunch with one of the key doctors on the staff. She said, "I really hate that letter. The hospital isn't like that. I wouldn't give to that appeal."

You succeed when you write letters that are appropriate to their audiences. I asked her, "Did you contribute to the staff appeal?" "Yes." "What did you think of that letter?" "Oh, it was all right." We had written the staff appeal, too, but written it doctor-to-doctor, so it had not seemed inappropriate to her. And so she gave.

STUDY UNIT

3

Never let a donor feel his or her response isn't essential

(Sample: year-end letter from a hospital)

(A) Dear Friend:

(B) Pre-Christmas is the time when most of us are considering our giving for the year. This letter is to ask that you include the Auburndale Medical Center in your planning.

(C) The Medical Center had a successful year last year, raising nearly $515,000. We are hopeful that we can surpass a $600,000 goal this year, and we need your help to do it.

(D) Please consider this as something more than a "run-of-the-mill" fund raising letter. The enclosed brochure documents many of the reasons our goal must be bigger. I sincerely hope you'll take a few minutes to read the brochure, not only because it identifies many of the items of physical equipment which our gifts will help to provide, but also because it tells a great deal about how important Auburndale Medical Center is to all of us, day in and day out.

(E) The Medical Center is truly a resource for our entire region. I personally like the idea that **(H)** my gift to the Medical Center stays right here in this area assisting not only the institutions of the Medical Center, but also our fellow citizens as well. I hope you will feel the same.

Please join me and hundreds of others in sending a thoughtful gift to the Medical Center. A contribution card and return envelope are enclosed for your convenience. On behalf of continued excellence at the Auburndale Medical Center, thank you.

Sincerely,

Signer
Position

Suggested Study Procedure

1. Read the letter straight through at your normal reading pace. Ask yourself, "Good, bad, or somewhere in between?"
2. Re-read the letter slowly.
3. Use the CopyRater™ to evaluate the letter in detail. Add your score. Then note the most important strengths and weaknesses.
4. Compare your ratings with the author's at the back of the workbook.
5. Read the essay at the end of this Study Unit.
6. Write the suggested Exercise material.
7. Review all the work, then add the most important idea(s) to your own developing personal list of letter-writing guidelines.

Exercises

1. Short of rewriting the entire letter, please correct the biggest single weakness you find in this letter.
2. Rewrite paragraph three to describe briefly one piece of equipment as an example for the whole replacement and updating process.
3. Alter next to last paragraph in letter body to replace "I personally like" notion with a more direct reason-to-contribute.

Comments on This Letter

(A) The "Dear Friend" salutation is the universal solvent for non-personalized direct mail. Nobody likes it much because it isn't true—if the person were a friend, you'd use his name. But nobody has invented a better general salutation. At least it's friendly! Some mailers make their first copy line a salutation, thus:

The Auburndale Medical Center
Needs 100 New Friends Because

(sentence continues in first paragraph of letter)

Not a bad technique. It starts the letter on a more urgent note than "Dear Friend." You might try this approach. If so, the main thing is to decide on something specific to ask for, then complete your ask in the opening lines of the first paragraph. Make it as clear and brief as possible.

(B) This lead paragraph is fairly good. "Pre-Christmas" could be written more simply. The passive voice, "This letter is to ask you . . ." should become an active "I'm writing this letter to ask you . . ." because the active voice is more vigorous and therefore more interesting. The underlying message in this paragraph—that the reader, like the letter-writer, is fairly well off—is flattering to the reader, and that's not bad. And the request is worded toward a serious gift, not a five dollar dismissive gift.

(C) I don't like this paragraph where it is. We've asked someone to support the Medical Center. His logical question is why? This paragraph should answer that question. What is the money needed for?

Let Self-Interest Motives Rule

My feeling about hospital appeals is that donors usually have strong self-interest motives for giving and these motives should be in the copy—e.g., "Your gift will help us equip the hospital to give you and your family the kind of care you need and deserve." (I've had better responses when I've asked for money for specific purposes rather than general needs, as in this letter. Perhaps we should all hang the motto, "Decide what you want most and ask for it" over our desks.)

(D) Easy reading is important. This paragraph is too long to be read easily. Don't let your paragraphs get over 5 lines long in a fund-raising letter. I'd certainly take the sentence, "Please consider this as something more than a run-of-the-mill fund raising letter," out. It's an editorial that adds nothing to the argument.

Instead of asking the reader to look at the brochure, I'd pick one piece of equipment, preferably one used in life-threatening situations, and describe it in the letter as an example of the hospital's needs.

(After many tests, I'm convinced the letter is where you win or lose because the donor makes up his mind when reading the letter whether to give or not. Other enclosures besides the letter should contain something that's very interesting and important to the appeal that cannot be described in the letter.)

(E) I like this paragraph, on the whole. It's personal and it provides two strong reasons to give—the more the better!

Gift Ranging to Increase Response

(F) This paragraph is okay, too, but I miss something important. People respond in greater numbers (donor prospects, I mean), if you offer them a range of specific suggested gifts to choose among. The suggested gift range is the business end of the letter—the bomb bay, if you like. The rest of the letter just gets you over your target.

There are many suggested gift techniques. In this case, I'd recommend a recitation of what other people have given—"To give you an idea what other friends have given, 000 people gave $100 to $1,000 or more last year, 000 people gave $25 to $100, and 000 people gave $25 or under. All gifts are deeply appreciated."

I've found that this suggested gift range, which is fairly aggressive (especially if most of your previous donors have given in the $10 to $15 range), doesn't decrease response noticeably. And people tend to give larger gifts, perhaps because they prefer to align themselves with the high-end donors. So it's a good prospecting gift range.

(G) I marked this closing paragraph because there is endless debate about who should sign fund-raising letters. This signer is not a hospital insider—the reference to "my own gift" makes that clear.

Unless you have a major celebrity with strong ties to your institution, the chief executive officer is usually your best signer. It is a big advantage to have the letter coming from the inside. Another important consideration in deciding who signs is quite pragmatic—who won't mess with your copy too much.

What's Missing?

(H) A P.S. should be here, but isn't. You use a P.S. because readers are believed to look at the lead paragraph to see if a letter is interesting (which is why your lead must be interesting!), then drop to the bottom to see how the letter ends.

Take advantage of this common reading pattern: use a P.S. in every letter for something important: a summary of your case, an expression of urgency, "We only have until March 5th to raise these crucial funds!" or an offer of personal recognition, "We'll be proud to add your name to our Honor Roll, published semi-annually in The Sentinel," or to point the reader at your enclosure, "As you can see from the enclosed photo, the foundations are down and the new church-hospital-wing-lodge-aquarium is well under way!"

Who's Getting This Letter?

One general point bothers me about this letter. I've read it several times, and though I have the impression it is aimed at wealthy persons who are non-donors, that's about all I can guess about the intended readers.

Who are they? Are they former patients? Do they live near the hospital? Do they have reason to know anything about the hospital? You always have some information about the lists you are mailing to, and you should use it in your letters if humanly possible.

In this case, if writing to a patient, you should say "As someone with recent firsthand experiences at the Medical Center . . ." If a nearby resident, "As someone who lives close to the hospital, you enjoy . . ." And so on. Such information *slants* the letter to the person at the other end. It's about him and therefore of interest to him.

It's a common mistake in direct mail to write a letter in such a way that it can be mailed efficiently to many different list segments and thereby cut printing costs. But that almost always makes a letter more bland, less personal, and more official-sounding—all of which hurts response.

4

A letter that looks hard to read probably won't be read

(Sample: children's camp appeal letter)

(A) CAMP AUBURNDALE is a non-profit summer camp for emotionally disturbed children and adolescents of Massachusetts. I'd like to tell you a little about our program and the children we serve.

(B) Erik is a 9 1/2 year old boy who lives in a public housing project with his mother and three brothers. Erik has a long history of loss and disappointments and is an angry young boy who feels he has no control over what happens to him. His father deserted the family many years ago and his mother spends many evenings working. Erik was referred to CAMP AUBURNDALE because of his angry outbursts and tantrums, inability to make and maintain friends, and suicidal attempts. Erik came to camp determined to convince all of us that we couldn't like him or care about him. Although long difficult days occurred, along with positive days, Erik was a different boy when summer ended. He learned that he was not as terrible as he thought he was, and that people could, and did, care about him. Erik made his first real set of friends this past summer. Follow up reports from Erik's teachers this fall tell us that his summer experience has made a vast difference. He is much more able, and willing, to learn, his peer relationships are now more positive and behavioral problems in the classroom have minimized.

(C) For CAMP AUBURNDALE to continue this valuable program, we need assistance from the business community in two major areas. The first is tuition aid for low income families, like Erik's. The cost of our eight week program is $760. Although our fee will remain the same for the 1982 season, state budget cuts have drastically reduced, and nearly eliminated, all previously available campership funding. We are asking the business community to fund a child for the 1982 summer, OR, to make a donation towards our second major area of need. This year the swimming pool **(D)** is in need of some major repairs, with estimated costs of $9,000. Supporters of this project will be publicly acknowledged, if they choose, at dedication ceremonies and their names will appear on a plaque at poolside.

(E) This is a nice way to show the community that you care about its children, AND, to get a tax deduction. If you have any questions about CAMP AUBURNDALE or the children in need of your assistance, PLEASE call me.

Thank you very much
Name, Position

Suggested Study Procedure

1. Read the letter straight through at your normal reading pace. Ask yourself, "Good, bad, or somewhere in between?"

2. Re-read the letter slowly.

3. Use the CopyRater™ to evaluate the letter in detail. Add your score. Then note the most important strengths and weaknesses.

4. Compare your ratings with the author's at the back of the workbook.

5. Read the essay at the end of this Study Unit.

6. Write the suggested Exercise material.

7. Review all the work, then add the most important idea(s) to your own developing personal list of letter-writing guidelines.

Exercises

1. Short of rewriting the entire letter, please correct the biggest single weakness you find in this letter.

2. Make Erik's story the lead—tell his story in the warmest, most personal, affecting way you can manage.

3. Then tell what the donor can do for the next "Erik."

Comments About This Letter

This letter soliciting funds from businesses came on a piece of stationery with an exceptionally deep masthead. Below that the name and address of the addressee was typed in. I think the letter has some good things in it, but the manner of presentation, produced here just as I read it, hurts it, possibly a great deal.

Let's talk about the visual problems. The lines are too long, the paragraphs are too long, and crowding the paragraphs is murder on the eye.

The eye "hops" along, reading phrases of several words at a time— fewer words or more words according to how good a reader you are.

Since we're trying to make our letters as easy as possible to read, we must try for material that read quickly, for lines that read easily. Here, every line in the letter is a visual *trudge:* It's hard work and very few readers work hard at reading!

Although the paragraphs are indented, there are no spaces between them, which creates a terribly uninviting mass.

The crowding was done to save using two sheets of paper for a letter whose natural length was probably about a page and a half. That saved a modest amount of money, but what if a couple of potential major donors didn't read it because it was so uninviting?

(A) Now go to paragraph one. I think the first sentence is good. It doesn't beat around the bush, it's businesslike (in a letter to businesses, that's good), and it provides an important fact. But I am not wild about the second sentence. The "I" is intrusive, and ". . . about our program and the children we serve suggests that the reader has something dull ahead.

Here is a revision of paragraph one that invites readers to go on:

"CAMP AUBURNDALE is a non-profit summer camp for emotionally disturbed Massachusetts youngsters. One of these children is an angry 9 1/2-year-old named Erik."

(B) Paragraph two tells Erik's story. This is exactly the right way to start Camp Auburndale's story. But the paragraph should be four paragraphs. It should include specific examples of Erik's growth. Phrases like "peer relationships" and "behavioral problems" should be replaced by simpler, warmer language.

These changes would give you a convincing story of how Camp Auburndale helped a troubled boy. But something's missing after paragraph two.

I want to know how many children like Erik come to the camp. I'd like more data on their home towns (to show the businesses that local children are there). I'd like more about camp activities. The letter should move from one child, Erik, to many children. And it doesn't, not in any direct way.

I'd want, too, to say that many children are able to camp as a result of camperships, whether governmental or private.

(C) The third paragraph, like the second, has good material but is too dense. I'd take it much more slowly, break it into briefer paragraphs. I would put the two requests directly to the individual businessman receiving the letter, thus:

"I hope your Company will consider underwriting a campership for a child this summer. We will send notices that you are sponsoring a child to area newspapers and stations (see draft). Partial camperships are very welcome, too."

(D) The swimming pool should get similar treatment in the next paragraph. Here I'd ask for a higher gift—perhaps $1,000—and offer even more in recognition, including the plaque, which I would describe.

(E) The fourth paragraph is friendly, brisk, direct, and aimed at reader interest. I wish there was urgency in it—indeed, in the entire letter. The sentence in the third paragraph that ends with ". . . state budget cuts . . ." hints the camp faces a serious financial problem. If so, say so. Tell how many children will be hurt. Say the reader has a major opportunity to help a child with serious problems.

This letter has good ingredients—a child's story, donor recognition, a large gift try. But it is short on emotional intensity and urgency. Even businessmen respond to emotional situations and want to feel needed.

STUDY UNIT

5

Using personalization effectively

(Sample: letter to veterans' auxiliary organization prospects)

Jane Smith
P.O. Box 187
Amherst, N.H. 03031

Dear Jane:

(A) Maybe you're like Bea Mooney. Bea didn't worry about veterans' benefits. That was her husband Charlie's business. Do you feel that way about Andrew's benefits? Woman to woman, Jane, I have to tell you that Bea darn near lost a farm that had been in her family for more than a century when Charlie died.

(B) If Bea had been a Vets Auxiliary member, things could have been different, Jane. She would have known that veterans' benefits involve her whole family, just as Andrew's benefits involve the whole Smith family. More important,

49

Bea would have known where to get the best help available—free help—when Charlie was gone.

This true story had a happy ending. A Vets National Service Officer came on the scene just in time to get the VA benefits Bea needed to save her family farm. And today Bea knows why DAV Auxiliary membership is so important—to her, and in just the same way, to you, Jane Smith.

(C) Two things will help the *Smith* family if trouble over VA benefits comes knocking on doors in Amherst . . First, the phone number of the Vets office in Amherst is 603-666-7664. The help is free. Second, by joining the Vets Auxiliary, you'll be kept informed about all the benefits Andrew has earned. Your membership will help us get the job done—for you and women like Bea.

(D) Jane, do it yourself and for the Smith family. Send in the form below with your $10.00 Auxiliary dues today. Do it now, while you're thinking about how much membership can mean to you!

Sincerely,
Name

Suggested Study Procedure

1. Read the letter straight through at your normal reading pace. Ask yourself, "Good, bad, or somewhere in between?"
2. Re-read the letter slowly.
3. Use the CopyRater™ to evaluate the letter in detail. Add your score. Then note the most important strengths and weaknesses.
4. Compare your ratings with the author's at the back of the workbook.
5. Read the essay at the end of this Study Unit.
6. Write the suggested Exercise material.
7. Review all the work, then add the most important idea(s) to your own developing personal list of letter-writing guidelines.

Exercises

1. Short of rewriting the entire letter, please correct the biggest single weakness you find in this letter.

2. Using the exact computer data used in this letter, write a brief letter for a women's college, one alumna to another.

Comments About This Letter

If we're going to study a computer-personalized letter, we might as well make it a doozy!

Here's a letter from the Auxiliary of a Veterans Organization to the wife of a ex-serviceman who is a member of the organization.

Purpose of the letter—to persuade her to join the auxiliary. Key selling point is the idea that she ought to know exactly what her husband's benefits are, because they involve the whole family. All other benefits are eliminated. The entire letter drives this point home.

An example—the unfortunate Bea, who almost lost the farm—is chosen to illustrate the importance of this one point.

What I want to study here is the merge of data from the data base to build a letter that feels very person-to-person—woman-to-woman, in fact.

If you looked at the original letter you would not have seen all the underlines, each of which is a merged bit of data. It looks more or less like a normal personal letter.

But the letter writer, after a careful scrutiny of the data base, chose to use the following data:

> *First and last name;*
> *Husband's first name;*
> *Street, City, State, ZIP;*
> *Location of nearest DAV office;*
> *Phone number for that office.*

In all, fifteen different line personalizations!

In donor prospecting, where you do not ordinarily have much data to use in personalizing, this letter may hold the record!

And it IS effective—it adds up to a letter that I believe would tend to keep a woman named Jane Smith reading from top to bottom, which means a large number of Jane Smiths will respond to the letter. If you can get everyone to read your letter you are virtually guaranteed a good response.

Some readers will quarrel with the extremely frequent use of "Jane" and "Jane Smith" on the ground that this isn't natural in a letter. That's true, and I'm not a tremendous fan of the frequent insertion of name personalization, but I do think that a person's name (imagine your name right here) can be used to draw a reader's eye to key points in your copy.

It's used here like a small bright flag, on the premise that no other word in the language is as interesting to someone as his or her name is.

In this letter the frequent repetitions of Bea, Bea Mooney, Charlie, her husband, seem to make it natural and logical to insert Jane, Jane Smith, and Andrew, her husband with equal frequency.

The copious use of both sets of names emphasizes the similarities between the two families, a key idea. Willy-nilly, this letter looks to me like the future of commercial and nonprofit direct mail, in which a skillful, experienced copywriter has picked up the available data and run with it to create a letter that is strong in all aspects and isn't just an old-style offset letter with personalization pasted into it.

We're already seeing extremely heavy use of personalization in sweepstakes and other commercial mail. The nonprofit world will not be far behind.

Now let's go through the personalizations.

(A) Here we have a good strong story lead, of special interest to the reader because it is closely related to her own family.

(B) This paragraph hits the key sales point—the DAV Auxiliary can tell you what your spouse's vets benefits are (is "even if he won't" implied here? I think so!).

(C) The DAV Service Officer saves the day!

(C) There's a DAV office very near you in (town) and the number is (phone). And the DAV Auxiliary "will keep you informed about the benefits Andrew has earned."

(D) Join for the good of your family. It's inexpensive. Do it now, while you think about it.

I've used the word "tight" before to describe certain letters, and I use it here. There are no distractions in this letter, it moves swiftly from point to point, closes, and stops. No flourishes and ruffles, no wasted words.

Donor Versus Prospect Letter Personalizing

Often, though not always, you don't have much data on file concerning your prospects—not, for example, as much as is shown in this letter. You are rarely going to have a spouse's name, for example, and putting in such data as the address of the nearest DAV office is something that had to be built in to the data just for this letter.

When there is little to use in the prospect file, go lightly in use of personalization. Every bit of data you add to a letter costs you money (or time, if you're word-processing in house). But donors are a different matter. Everything you do in a letter that shows you relate to a donor on a one-to-one basis confirms the donor's feeling that he or she is doing the right thing in supporting your organization.

That's why you want to use the last gift if you can, why you use gift data, a first name, a family name, and anything else that shows the donor you are aware of him or her as an individual. And to show the donor that you do keep track of his or her gift.

Many direct mail programs I've been involved in have followed the general tactic of mailing offset, or very modestly personalized, letters to prospects, then adding donors who give more than a certain minimum amount to the donor base and mailing only personalized mail to them thereafter.

This is a good approach because it minimizes your cost-per-letter in prospecting (which in turn makes it possible for you to mail more widely) and increases your donor's sense that he or she is personally and individually important to you.

STUDY UNIT
6

Why you must get better at direct mail—the competition is brutal

(Sample: letter to high school alumni/alumnae)

Auburndale Memorial Field Restoration Committee

Dear Alumnus/Alumna:

(A) Among Auburndale High School's greatest resources are the loyal alumni/alumnae who demonstrate on many occasions how highly they value the education which they received at Auburndale.

(B) Because you are one of the loyal alumni/alumnae, we ask you to translate appreciation of your education at Auburndale into a contribution for our Memorial Field Restoration Project.

(C) A combined Auburndale High School Boosters Group has been organized to help raise funds for the restoration of Memorial Field. The City has asked us to show community concern and support for the project by raising funds for the "little extras" that will make the field complete. We need lights, a concession stand, a scoreboard, bleachers, and a running, jumping, and throwing area to complement the renovation of the football/soccer field and practice track. Also included in the renovation is necessary underground wiring and plumbing.

(D) Your assistance will make a positive impact. Your check will help us to support the nearly 600 students who actively use the field, including football players, soccer players, track and field participants, cheerleaders, and the Deering Marching Band.

(E) Your contribution will ensure that Auburndale will continue to support quality education both in academics and in extracurricular activities. Please be loyal to the Purple and White by sending your gift today. We must attain our goal soon, so please make out your tax-exempt check to: Memorial Field Committee.

(F) We extend our sincere appreciation for your gracious support of Auburndale High School.

Sincerely,

Name

P.S. The names of all donors will be included on the scoreboard. Here's your chance to earn a bit of immortality.

Suggested Study Procedure

1. Read the letter straight through at your normal reading pace. Ask yourself, "Good, bad, or somewhere in between?"

2. Re-read the letter slowly.

3. Use the CopyRater™ to evaluate the letter in detail. Add your score. Then note the most important strengths and weaknesses.

4. Compare your ratings with the author's at the back of the workbook.

5. Read the essay at the end of this Study Unit.

6. Write the suggested Exercise material.

7. Review all the work, then add the most important idea(s) to your own developing personal list of letter-writing guidelines.

Exercises

1. Short of rewriting the entire letter, please correct the biggest single weakness you find in this letter.

2. Revise the "ask" to include (and make a strong pitch to) people who normally give in the $25-plus range as well as higher levels. Use three paragraphs for this (don't worry about letter length).

Comments About This Letter

We talk about the increasing competition for direct mail dollars, but this letter sends a gentle chill up my spine.

My partner received it from her high school—a public high school, by the way, tax-supported, et cetera. It's a bit surprising to see a direct mail appeal coming from a public high school.

Everybody is in the mail these days!

But that's not the source of the chill.

No, I'm fascinated by the presence in this letter of so many professional response techniques. It's not a perfect letter, but it is by no means a bad one either!

Well, so what? It shows how stiff the competition is getting, that's what!

(A) The lead (really, the first two paragraphs) is a pretty good attempt to make the donor feel important.

(B) The "ask" begins early and is very clear and specific.

(C) Although slightly funny—if the list of items needed is the "little extras" what's left for the city to do? This is a good, detailed paragraph. Specific needs always beat generalities!

(D) Very strong "you" paragraphs here, always good for reader interest.

(E) States the broader goals well, stresses loyalty, asks for money now and tells where to send the money (a reply envelope was also included).

(F) Excellent P.S. A strong offer of recognition linked to a large gift. "Here's your chance to purchase a bit of immortality"—what a good line!

Throughout, the letter contains few wasted words and no ideas that are not relevant to the case for a gift—the only proper subject of a direct mail letter.

You see an attempt to connect the person who is reading to the high school, a specific request, the specific equipment needs, the many young people who will benefit, and as noted above, the broader goals. The case is really complete.

I don't say this letter is inspiring, but the plain truth about direct mail fund-raising is that not many letters are inspired or inspiring. Specific common-sense goals and a low-key, logical approach get consistently good responses for you.

Some Criticisms

I thought the lead was okay, though the weakest part of the letter and more wordy than it needs to be. The following would have done as well and got the reader to your point quickly:

"As a loyal graduate of Auburndale, you should be aware of a major restoration of Memorial Field that's about to take place. What's more, we hope you'll play a part in it."

The lady who got this letter will probably contribute, but didn't like the lead and thought it was a serious problem.

She felt that since she hadn't lived in "Auburndale" since she was a girl and had never been called on by the high school for anything, it was phony to spend so much time on what a great resource the alumni were. It was a real turn-off for her.

We had a slight disagreement over this. I felt that the basic thought of the lead was a good one, but as often happens, the writer got carried away trying to explain what it meant.

If he or she had said, for instance, "When you were at Auburndale it counted on your loyalty, and it's counting on you today,"

I think the key point would have been made.

My other criticism of this letter is that the reply slip (not shown) only has one suggested gift—$500. I don't think it's ever a good idea to ask for just one gift. In this case, a casual reading suggests only $500 is being sought. You can eliminate a lot of gifts very easily this way!

An Excellent Enclosure

Though I can't show it here, the letter was accompanied by a reprint of a sports column from an area newspaper: "Night football could be on way back at Auburndale."

That's a good addition to the package. It has credibility because it comes from an outside source, the newspaper, and it goes into more detail about the restoration of the field, the fund-raising program, and the need for lights.

A Good Reply Vehicle

The wallet-flap reply envelope in the package was good, too. It carried this headling: "YES, I want to help insure the success of AUBURNDALE MEMORIAL FIELD's restoration."

That's a good use of the "YES" technique that is widely believed to increase response when it appears in big bold letters on your reply slip or envelope. The suggested gift array included $10, $25 and $100 suggestions as well as larger ones. The envelope had a question about Class Year and offered a chance to volunteer.

In Conclusion

This letter shows you that many people are learning the basic techniques of good direct mail fund-raising letter-writing—which means that in order to compete effectively, you have to be skilled in this area, too.

And speaking of competition—your real competitors in direct mail fund-raising are not the museum around the corner or the hospital down the street. They are the fund-raising letters that reach someone the same day yours does.

Those are the ones your package has to beat. And since so many are highly professional these days, you need to use the things in direct mail that are known to work well.

STUDY UNIT

7

When premiums help or fail to help response— giveaways and fund raising

(Sample: prospecting letter for conservation agency—this came with a series of commemorative wildlife stamps)

Dear Fellow Citizens:

(A) The conservation organization I invite you to join with a special contribution is by no means the largest.

(B) But the committed group of men and women you'll be joining when you do, have been responsible—over the course of 50 years—for saving millions of acres of wilderness . . . specifically beautiful, irreplaceable areas that might otherwise have been lost forever.

To celebrate that 50 year effort, I'm sending you a series of commemorative stamps—each representing some of the land The Auburndale Society has fought so hard to protect.

These beautiful, specially designed stamps serve to recognize 50 years of devoted dedicated work toward the protection and preservation of America's wilderness.

They are our 50th anniversary gift to you.

I hope you'll enjoy and use them as a striking and decorative touch for your letter and packages and as quiet testimony to our commonly held belief that America needs wilderness.

Indeed, it's that very strong and firmly held belief that motivates us to continue the work on behalf of this country's wild places with an even greater sense of urgency.

For America does need her wilderness and unless you and I take action today, that need will go unfulfilled for future generations of Americans . . . for your grandchildren and mine . . . in the next 50 years and beyond.

This organization—The Auburndale Society— now faces its greatest challenges ever. So on behalf of the entire membership and Governing Council, I call upon you to help us meet those challenges.

(C) Today, The Auburndale Society is one of America's most effective and respected conservation organizations. Our membership is 125,000 strong. We are the only national conservation organization that concentrates all its energies and resources on the preservation and wise management of the public lands.

We need to protect these areas from being bulldozed, stripmined, denuded and drilled.

Once these wild lands are lost, they are gone forever.

The majesty of some of our most precious lands is being sacrificed so that oil can be extracted from the land and strip mining can be carried out without adequate safeguards to protect the environment.

We have our work cut out for us . . . saving forest areas and other public lands. The land that was not set aside as wilderness can still be protected for enjoyment for the public. There can be a balanced approach that takes into account the public interest. The fate of forest areas depends on our alerting the public to what is happening.

We are fortunate here in the United States to have some of the most beautiful wilderness areas in the world.

Destroy them and you destroy our spirit . . . destroy them and you destroy our sense of values . . . destroy them and you deprive future generations of the greatest heritage . . . destroy them and you upset a critical balance of nature, an upset that will have long-range adverse effects on our health and quality of life.

Wilderness and the environment have become today's scapegoat, sacrificed on the altar of economic expediency. The goals of the development interests that would see our wilderness areas destroyed are expedient—but shortsighted.

They will reap their profits and we may have more timber, oil, and minerals . . . momentarily. But then what? If we strip our forests, where will tomorrow's timber come from? If we destroy wildlife habitats, what will happen to our animals? If we pollute our air and water, what will happen to our health?

Your gift could well be one of the best investments you've ever made. And the beautiful stamps I've enclosed can serve as a reminder of that investment.

I hope you'll enjoy them and will use your stamps as a gentle testimony to our shared belief that America needs her wilderness . . . and to show you support our work.

We have 50 years of success behind us, but miles and acres to go in preserving the wilderness that is such an important part of our American heritage.

Please help us. Send your tax-deductible gift today.

Sincerely,

Name
Position

P.S. For a $20 contribution, we will send you four free issues (one every three months) of the spectacularly beautiful magazine, Wilderness. See enclosed contribution form.

Suggested Study Procedure

1. Read the letter straight through at your normal reading pace. Ask yourself, "Good, bad, or somewhere in between?"
2. Re-read the letter slowly.
3. Use the CopyRater™ to evaluate the letter in detail. Add your score. Then note the most important strengths and weaknesses.
4. Compare your ratings with the author's at the back of the workbook.
5. Read the essay at the end of this Study Unit.
6. Write the suggested Exercise material.
7. Review all the work, then add the most important idea(s) to your own developing personal list of letter-writing guidelines.

Exercises

1. Short of rewriting the entire letter, please correct the biggest single weakness you find in this letter.
2. Rewrite this letter to eliminate any generalizations you find meaningless or dull. Replace them with specifics (you can invent them) that demonstrate need for conservation.
3. Write a lead that would slant this letter to a current member.

Comments About This Letter

This prospect mailing for The Auburndale Society, a well-known conservation organization, began well but got off course.

On the outside envelope, to the left of the window, are two black and white photos of their stamps.

Below them, writ large, "Your FREE American Wilderness Stamps . . . see enclosed."

Good start because such stamps—Easter Seals, Christmas Seals, Wilderness Stamps, National Wildlife Federation, et cetera—increase response.

The theory is if you give people a front-end premium (the stamps), they will feel obligated to send a contribution.

Personally, I don't think stamps work that way. I think people just plain like stamps and are more inclined to open an envelope with stamps in it. If more people open the envelope, more people will send contributions because the mailer has gotten more people to consider its appeal.

Whether I'm right or wrong, the idea that people might feel obligated to respond to the "present" of stamps was clearly the guiding idea in this mailing. It was also the only idea.

Let's look at the letter. If you have a teaser offer on the outside envelope your lead should flow from the teaser. Here, it would have been a good idea to print in boldface above the "Dear Fellow Citizen."

> USE THE ENCLOSED WILDERNESS STAMPS TO HELP THE AUBURNDALE SOCIETY CELE- BRATE 50 YEARS OF SAVING WILDLANDS— AND JOIN US IN THE LAND SAVING BATTLES AHEAD!

In that way you quickly make Point #1—we're giving you something and Point #2—we're asking you to save wild land.

(A) Why would you begin an appeal with a negative point about your organization? This is the lead paragraph, the most crucial moment in the prospects' "thumbs up/thumbs down" decision on whether to read your letter—and it's just here that the writer chose to say ". . . by no means the largest."

(B) This is of minimal interest to readers because it isn't about the reader, and this is a difficulty that runs throughout the letter, which is almost entirely about the organization.

The writing isn't bad, but the reader isn't getting any details. He isn't told exactly what the Auburndale Society does, or how it does it. He doesn't know what land it has saved. He doesn't know what the 125,000 members do—and isn't being invited to join them, anyway, but merely to send a gift.

I say "merely" advisedly. I can't understand why an organization with a wonderfully attractive name (the real name of the Society) wouldn't use prospect mailings to build its membership, reckoning that additional support is much, MUCH easier to get from members than from outsiders.

If this were a membership package, the Society could have stressed the benefits of membership. But as it reads, a straight request for a gift, no benefits, they should have and failed to present a specific, important, action-now kind of case, with a clear danger and a good solution that required the prospects's help.

I really didn't find such a case here. Perhaps the Society felt just mailing the stamps was enough, but you don't get prospects to come over to your side by explaining the many reasons you deserve support. You get prospects to join you by offering them an exciting, interesting problem to solve, worthwhile parts to play, recognition.

(C) This paragraph contains the letter's second specific fact—the Society's 125,000 members.

Take a deep breath. You will now read to the end of the letter more than a page away, and not encounter any more actual facts.

You will find a nicely written well-reasoned appeal without meat. Nothing says "look, you can take a giant step toward solving this serious problem."

I found a hint of something that could have been a strong appeal, namely that the Society watchdogs government management of public lands.

No one interested in conservation believes the government is managing public lands well. So the Society might have made an urgent case for the need to stand watch. But the case had to be put is a vivid, specific way, if possible with localizing example.

(I think of The Nature Conservancy, an organization that does super direct mail, and how it once used the computer to fill in specific Conservancy projects in each reader's home state or region. It was a brilliant example of using the computer and personalization data to bringing an appeal "home" to a reader. It raised lots of money and won a national award.)

Summary

My subjective evaluation parallels my numerical rating—the stamps were a good idea, the 50th year is a good moment for growth*, but so many other opportunities to be specific, offer membership benefits, build a vital, real case, show, not tell, were passed over that this mailing makes me feel a bit sad. Because this is a good cause.

I felt "pressure from above" the development office in almost every line—don't tell them how much we need them, tell them how much they need us.

Nothing wrecks a mailing faster than being written to please a leadership that is only interested in the organization and won't think about what makes people tick. Or respond.

Comment: The Stamps

Once inside the package the first thing I did was look for the stamps. And what did I see? They gave me ten stamps but used the whole top row (five more potential stamps) for text—important to them, but of minimal interest to me. Better to have printed more stamps? The text could have been on the reverse side.

Production Comment: The Paper

The letter ran the front and back of one page, but also used an additional sheet for one more line of text, the signature, and the P.S. That means the organization doubled its paper cost to print one line of persuasion! If the quantity mailed was huge, and it probably was, they spent many thousands of dollars for that one extra line of copy.

In the earlier discussion of CAMP AUBURNDALE I suggested that the physical crowding of most of two pages of text onto one sheet hurt response. Here the reverse mistake was made—this letter was very "cuttable" but the organization chose to add a lot of cost for no response-based reason that I can see.

* It is an odd but often-demonstrated fact that special anniversary years of organizations, 25th, 50th, and so on, if given strong play in direct mail, have a good impact on prospects and donors, especially the latter.

I've found that any anniversary year divisible by 5—10th, 15th, 20th, 25th, et cetera—tends to help response if you refer to it in the right way.

Here's the right way: "Won't you help us celebrate this very special 35th Anniversary of the Children's Home by sending a specially generous gift?" I always look to see how old an organization is when I'm writing for it.

8

How self-conscious copy lowers response

(Sample: prospect letter for a hospital)

(A) Dear Patients and Friends:

(B) Some people disregard our Annual Giving Appeal for financial aid to the hospital because they think such requests are really intended for people who give big gifts.

Before you disregard this appeal, would you think with me for just a minute about why you might spare a few dollars.

It is not pleasant to be hospitalized, but even worse to become "medically indigent." We certainly don't intend to become ill, but, in spite of all our planning, a serious illness or extended hospital stay often has drastic effects on our financial resources.

Many people, like you and I, are faced with this problem each year. As a result, Auburndale Hospital spends many thousands of dollars every year to provide care for those unable to pay.

It is only the generosity of thoughtful people like you that enables us to defray these costs. This once-a-year help makes the purchase of vital equipment possible—equipment that saves lives.

(C) Now that you have read this far, please reflect on our need for your support. Include this letter with **(D)** your monthly bills, and when you start writing checks for the mortgage, gas, electricity, etc., please consider writing one more check for Auburndale Hospital—no matter what the amount. For your convenience, we have enclosed a partial list of important equipment to which your gift may be applied.

(E) I can sincerely assure you of the warmest thanks from those who are patients in the Hospital, as well as those of us who are closely involved with its fine work.

(F) Sincerely,   **(F)** Sincerely,

Name   Name
Position   Position

(G)

Suggested Study Procedure

1. Read the letter straight through at your normal reading pace. Ask yourself, "Good, bad, or somewhere in between?"
2. Re-read the letter slowly.
3. Use the CopyRater™ to evaluate the letter in detail. Add your score. Then note the most important strengths and weaknesses.
4. Compare your ratings with the author's at the back of the workbook.
5. Read the essay at the end of this Study Unit.
6. Write the suggested Exercise material.
7. Review all the work, then add the most important idea(s) to your own developing personal list of letter-writing guidelines.

Exercises

1. Short of rewriting the entire letter, please correct the biggest single weakness you find in this letter.

2. Write a lead and second paragraph that would strongly slant this letter to a former patient. Get the need for his or her help going right away.

3. Replace the need here to help those unable to pay with something of more interest to a former patient—a piece of equipment, for instance, that would be used to save lives.

Comments About This Letter

This letter, although by no means terrible, does contain some clear-cut no-no's.

(A) Starting with the dual salutation. The idea here was to make one print job work over two lists—the former patient list and what in all likelihood is called the "house list," i.e. the potpourri of Board, medical staff, staff, trustees, names-from-nowhere, and donors, who really must get letters strongly rooted in their special status if you want to keep renewing them.

In addition to not sending special letters to donors, there was another cost to this cost-cutting—giving up the one-to-one mode of address that is absolutely basic to direct mail fund-raising letters.

(A) The moment a plural salutation appears, it tells readers, this is going to a lot of people (So how much will it matter if I don't read it?). It tells readers you don't know exactly whether he is a friend or a patient (So how much do they care about me if they don't even know who I am?).

This alone wouldn't wreck response to a strong letter, but most letters are not strong, they are by definition average in the response they get, and in an average letter, every negative jumps out at readers and reduces response.

(B) This paragraph is a response killer. The thought is much too complicated for direct mail. Stop a bit and read what it actually says:

> "Some people disregard our Annual Giving Appeal . . ." (!!!)

If this letter was a computer program, your screen would be saying Fatal Error about now. People will take anything you write in a letter at its face value. If you suggest that some people don't give, you'll probably find that a lot of people don't give. There is a classic "band wagon" approach that works in direct mail. "So many of your friends and neighbors have donated because they know the Hospital is really important to everyone who lives on Lake Avenue. I thought you might well feel the same, so I've enclosed an envelope . . ." The lead in this letter is the exact opposite.

(B) Something else bothers me: the phrase, ''. . . you might spare a few dollars?'' That has an overly casual tone. It downplays the value of a small gift.

Big gifts or small, every donor thinks what he or she has sent is important. Once I wrote: ''You might think a gift like your last one of $000 is not enough by itself to make any difference . . .''

The organization was swamped with letters from angry donors, all saying, ''What do you MEAN my gift doesn't make any difference?!''

So ''spare a few dollars'' sent the letter in a bad direction. The main point of any letter to any donor should be how important the donor's help has been, is now, and will ever be.

(C) Here we have another kind of problem, a non sequitur. Every paragraph in a letter must flow out of the idea of the preceding one. This one heads off in a new direction, and is connected back only vaguely in the long following paragraph.

A bridge sentence was needed. Could have been something like this: ''Here's one reason I hope you'll send a contribution: Agnes J., or anyone else who needs its care. It's the philosophy of this hospital to cure the sick, not to make money.''

''And that's why we depend on the help of so many of our good neighbors who look to the Auburndale for care.''

''They—and you too, I hope—send what they can when they can, large gifts and small. And it all helps!''

Well, I went far beyond a ''bridge sentence.''

But perhaps the above shows you the problem with the letter exists throughout it. It's not human enough.

(C) I don't like ''Now that you have read this far,'' which gave me the feeling I was being watched.

(D) And the suggestion the letter be put away until bill paying time rather than acted on now is daring. I don't think I've ever seen that idea before. But it's not logical. You really want people to take action now, not later, and especially not later at bill paying time!

It's somewhat lazy to put in a list of equipment needs and let the reader make a choice. What works better for me is to take one or two examples of equipment needs and develop it or them as being typical of the hospital's overall needs.

There is no suggested gift array in the letter, which is a mistake second only to a bad lead in importance. At best, the reader is left wondering what would be an appropriate gift. A wondering donor is a likely non-donor.

(E) This last paragraph should have been eliminated. It says little, doesn't contribute to the argument, isn't believable.

''. . . the warmest thanks from those who are patients in the hospital . . .''

72

(F) I'm not a fan of multiple signature letters, because they are harder to write informally, and informality is very important in fund-raising copy.

(G) Where's the P.S.? It's a high readership point, so you can add substance to a letter with a P.S. You could offer a premium, ''For $25 we'll send you an expedited admissions card.'' You can add urgency. You can restate your premise concisely. You can offer the donor a place on your Honor Roll. Et cetera.

STUDY UNIT

9

Lead with your biggest idea

(Sample: public television letter to prospects)

Dear Friend:

(A) You tune to Channel 1 for outstanding programs—not pledge drives. Yet I know you understand our need to encourage support from our viewers. And right now we need that support more than ever.

(B) At this point in 1984 we face a serious financial challenge—we are 19% below our fund raising goal. Our financial health, and the programs you enjoy, may suffer if we carry this burden throughout the winter. We are making every effort to get back on target, and I hope that we can count on your extra support at this time.

(C) Our March pledge drive on Channel 1 is scheduled to air from the 3rd through the 18th. This traditional fund raising effort will bring in many new contributors, but it will not be enough to compensate for the shortfall.

(D) Your extra gift of $100, $35, $50 or any amount will bring us within reach of our financial target. It will also give us a headstart on our March pledge drive.

(E) Because you're such a special friend, I want to share with you the enclosed memo which lists the program schedule with actual start times during the March drive. This way, you can enjoy the spectacular programming without the fund raising.

Please help us get back on financial target by sending the largest gift you can in the enclosed envelope. Your generosity, as well as your program comments, will be most welcome and appreciated. Thank you!

Sincerely,

Name
Position

Suggested Study Procedure

1. Read the letter straight through at your normal reading pace. Ask yourself, "Good, bad, or somewhere in between?"
2. Re-read the letter slowly.
3. Use the CopyRater™ to evaluate the letter in detail. Add your score. Then note the most important strengths and weaknesses.
4. Compare your ratings with the author's at the back of the workbook.
5. Read the essay at the end of this Study Unit.
6. Write the suggested Exercise material.
7. Review all the work, then add the most important idea(s) to your own developing personal list of letter-writing guidelines.

Exercises

1. Short of rewriting the entire letter, please correct the biggest single weakness you find in this letter.
2. Revise this lead to talk about the enclosed TV schedule, but follow through immediately and strongly on the need for help, linking the two in a natural, easy way.

3. This letter only says the station needs money. Add a paragraph to show the donor why the money would be a good investment.

Comments About This Letter

Got a letter from our public television channel recently. The envelope was brown with large red letters that said "IMPORTANT NOTICE. OPEN AT ONCE!"

I can't quote response statistics on this, but personally I don't respond well to commands from envelopes, especially from an organization that's about to ask for money.

Inside, though, a pleasant surprise. The enclosure that came with the letter was a memo of the actual starting times of the station's programs during the station's upcoming pledge drive.

For anyone who watches public television frequently, that's a good piece of information to receive.

It accomplishes three things: It is a useful premium that treats the donor as an insider and is therefore flattering; it will help keep people watching despite the interminable on-air fund-raising; and like any schedule, it is a device for promoting the station's programs—to the station's best audience.

In other words, that was a heck of a good idea!

But shouldn't the schedule have been mentioned on the outside envelope? Like this?

"Dear Donor, I've enclosed a schedule of the real starting times of all programs during our March 3–18 pledge drive."

That would guarantee that the envelope would be opened, I should think, and that's what a teaser is supposed to accomplish.

(A) Now let's look at the letter. Is the schedule mentioned in the lead paragraph? No, it seems to say something rather obvious, a negative, in fact, that is better unsaid.

(B) Is the schedule mentioned in paragraph two? No, this appears to be the actual beginning of the fund-raising appeal. It would have made a perfectly respectable, though unexciting, lead paragraph.

(C) This third paragraph continues the request. Reasonable, sensible, direct. But still no mention of the premium.

(D) The fourth paragraph is too vague for my taste (in addition to not mentioning the premium). The station knows what I gave and when I last gave it and it is using full personalization.

Why not, "Mr. Squires, we have missed your assistance a great deal since you sent a gift of $000 back in 19XX. Won't you equal that gift, or send a gift of any size that's possible for you, now?"

Or if I were a recent donor, why not, "Mr. Squires, we were extremely pleased that you chose to send that generous gift of 000 last October. To minimize the need for on air pledging and keep our program level high, won't you make a stretch and send a gift of $000 or even $000 or more now—and become a member of our Leaders Club?" (or what-you-will).

(E) Now we reach the paragraph I think should have been the lead. It is a valid reward, it is useful, and it is a great way to begin a fund-raising appeal. After leading with this paragraph, the writer could have followed with something like this:

> "I hope you'll place the memo near your set and use it to avoid what I know is tedious time for people like yourself who give so generously and regularly."
>
> "And won't you do one thing more? Help us get the pledge period off to the best possible start— one that will make up any current deficit in our fund-raising goal and help us plan even shorter pledge periods in the future?"
>
> "What you could do, and it would be a tremendous help, is to consider whether it is possible to increase your last gift of $000 this spring to one of $000 or $000 or even more."

This letter was pretty good, by and large, but when you come up with an idea for a premium that's an absolute natural, that is certain to be well received, that ties as directly to your appeal as this one did, don't bury it, lead with it.

It's good to remember before mailing a letter, although you personally are more interested in the parts of the letter are about your organization, the donor or prospect is more interested in the parts of the letter about him or her—and since the reader's convenience is served by a schedule that helps eliminate the downtime of waiting for pledging to be over, it is a decisive step in the right direction.

When in doubt about whether you've taken the right line in a letter or not, always go in the direction of enlarging the parts that are about the reader. You increase reader interest by doing that.

STUDY UNIT

10

The thank you to a major donor— how to write a great one and why it matters so much

(Sample: thank you letter to a conservation donor)

Dear Name,

On behalf of Auburndalepeace, I wish to thank you for your donation of $100.00 to our work. We need the support of individuals such as yourself in working for a safe, clean environment.

For the upcoming year, Auburndalepeace will be focussing on two major environmental problems—the poisoning of our land and waters by toxic wastes, and the protection of endangered marine mammal wildlife. Toxic pollution remains one of the largest problems facing the United States today. Each year over 250 million tons of toxic waste are generated by industry— enough for one ton of each and every American alive today. Current disposal methods are inadequate for treating these wastes, and the laws regulating disposal are weak or non-existent. Auburndalepeace calls for source reduction as the solution to this serious problem. Technology exists today for the substitution of non-toxic materials in manufacturing processes, for profitable recycling of waste products, and for the elimination of unnecessary waste production in industry.

At the beginning of 1985, the Japanese government announced it would defy the International Whaling Commission ban on the hunting of sperm whales. The United States, as a member of the IWC, is legally bound to enforce sanctions against Japanese fishing rights in American coastal waters. After meeting with Japanese negotiators, the United States government decided not to impose any sanctions. In response, Auburndalepeace has joined fourteen other environmental and conservation groups in filing a motion of summary judgment against the U.S. Department of Commerce and State to force American complicance with the IWC ruling and invoke fishing sanctions against the Japanese. In addition, sixteen international environmental organizations have joined together in an economic boycott of Japanese Government-owned Japan Air Lines (JAL) to publicly show the worldwide oppostion to Japan's decision to resume hunting sperm whales.

Again, thank you for your support. I will keep you informed about Auburndalepeace's efforts in the upcoming year. Please call me if there are any questions you might have about Auburndalepeace. If you are ever in the area, feel free to drop in and see our office.

Sincerely,

Name
Position

Suggested Study Procedure

1. Read the letter straight through at your normal reading pace. Ask yourself, "Good, bad, or somewhere in between?"
2. Re-read the letter slowly.

3. Use the CopyRater™ to evaluate the letter in detail. Add your score. Then note the most important strengths and weaknesses.

4. Compare your ratings with the author's at the back of the workbook.

5. Read the essay at the end of this Study Unit.

6. Write the suggested Exercise material.

7. Review all the work, then add the most important idea(s) to your own developing personal list of letter-writing guidelines.

Exercises

1. Short of rewriting the entire letter, please correct the biggest single weakness you find in this letter.

2. Do some serious simplifying and re-paragraphing of this letter without losing the "you are an insider" approach.

Comments About This Letter

Here's a letter that came as a thank you for a good-sized gift.

The envelope was closed-face and the letter is word-processed. I suspect I was addressed as "Con" because the computer could not figure out whether the salutation sould be Mr., Ms. or what, and went to a non sex-biased alternative.

In general, I don't hold with the idea of jumping onto a first name basis in this way—maybe that's just New England reserve showing, though.

I like the agency and am able to contribute at a level that gets me classed as a major donor, which I mention here only because that status dictated the approach and tone of the letter.

It is the kind of thank you an agency sends to a major donor—it pays me the compliments of:

> *A. Assuming that I am an intelligent and serious person (ha!);*
> *B. Am seriously interested in conservation;*
> *C. Do not need information "simplified" to understand it.*

It is, in short, the kind of letter you would send to someone whom you perceive to be an ally, someone whom you were welcoming into a cause and whom you feel has a serious commitment.

Now I might be all of A, B, and C above, or I might not be, but it makes ALL KINDS of sense for the agency to address me in this way. It is flattering. It is informative.

It is, in my opinion, the kind of letter they should send to every donor—not necessarily word-processed, just the basic text. Because it is the kind of letter that might lift a few people who do not yet have a major commitment into a higher level of participation the next time an appeal arrives. Listen, within the limits of your budget, why not write to everybody as a major donor? All it costs is a few adjectives! And everybody perceives himself or herself to be providing major help whether sending $5 or $5000.

The letter says good things about the organization by the same process of being serious and by not making the problems ahead seem easier to solve than they really are. This letter is realistic, and that supports the reader's impression of the sincerity of the organization.

Actually, the letter is more clear about what the agency is doing and plans to do in relation to whales, its traditional cause, than in the discussion of toxic pollution.

But that's understandable, because nobody really seems to know what to do about toxic pollution when you come right down to it.

The paragraphs are too long, however. I don't really think any letter writer would set about to make it actively hard for a reader, but 17–18 line paragraphs do just that, especially when the type is small and the lines are long.

The closing is extremely personable and friendly. It invites me to drop in for a visit, and it does NOT ask me for another gift right now.

You ask at your peril when you are writing to people who have just given you what they regard as substantial gifts.

A wealthy friend once told me about a national health agency she had given to. She said she gave two hundred dollars. She didn't hear a word for two months, then got a letter that said, in effect, ''Thanks a lot, that was great, can you send $400 this time?

The thank you was a good idea, and the agency might have included an extra gift envelope, but such an upgrade suggestion to a new major donor bordered on idiotic.

You know how agencies make decisions like that? They completely forget people are on the other end—anyone with a lick of sense would have seen that was a bad tactic.

(This irritated lady, who was a millionaire, later died of cancer. Is there much likelihood that her grieving family would support the health agency that sent her that thank you letter?)

I suggest to Auburndalepeace that it print an offset version of this exact letter—on one sheet, front and back, if necessary, and mail it to all recent donors. It would tend to have as good an effect on a $25 donor as it does on a $100 donor. And we have seen in direct mail fund-raising again and again that many well-to-do people ''test the water'' with small gifts to see how an agency will respond before they send larger gifts. They may be doing this already, of course.

There is one more bit of segmentation I would recommend here: a special version to first-time donors that begins by thanking them particularly for deciding to support the work of the agency at this time. Praise the decision to act as much or more than you do the contribution itself. Why? Because all the tests show that one-time donors renew less well than multi-gift donors, and this is just one more way to increase the odds that a first-time donor will renew.

Few agencies like to do thank you letters—they don't provide income and they are time consuming. But they do have a positive impact on renewals, which are what direct mail fund-raising is all about. Prospecting is where you try to find as many new friends as possible. Renewals are where the real money is.

STUDY UNIT

11

Copy overkill— how to lose a reader's interest in a hurry

(Sample: prospect letter to former patients in a hospital)

Dear Former Patient:

(A) Time has slipped by quickly since you were a patient at Auburndale Hospital. Since the day you returned home, thousands of others have also gone home, to take up their lives in our community. People including little Candy Turner.

(C) Candy was just 6 when her left arm was severed in a car crash. She was then rushed to Auburndale Hospital, where a team of surgeons worked all night to reattach her arm. The process they used to achieve this modern miracle is called microsurgery. Today, Candy has use of both arms, thanks to helping hands across our state.

(B) Our physicians and staff have seen miracles happen over and over, due in part to some of the newest, finest medical equipment. To purchase such equipment, we've depended in part on generous gifts made by friends from all over this area . . . many of whom are former patients like you.

A powerful surgical microscope helped doctors save Candy's arm. It was made possible by the wonderful generosity of such friends. Other examples:

(C) A man we'll call Arthur was rushed here last year with severe chest pains. A cardiac examination showed he needed by-pass surgery and that special treatment would be needed to keep him alive until his operation. Gifts had helped purchase an intra-aortic balloon pump. Inserted into Arthur's heart, it kept his heart beating until surgery could be done.

No age group is immune to diseases that require immediate and continuing use of sophisticated and expensive machines.

(C) (A third story, the medical care given to a girl named Sandra, suffering from kidney failure in her mid-twenties, appeared here in the letter. Its length was about equal to Cindy's story.)

There are so many more Candys and Arthurs and Sandras. Perhaps you were one of them at one time . . . and perhaps your life was saved because Auburndale Hospital had the equipment you needed when you needed it.

(D) Could it now be your turn to pass along the gift of life to others with your generosity?

(E) You can help! Your gift, no matter how modest, could enable us to buy some life-giving piece of equipment we desperately need.

(F) Your gift for others makes you feel good too. There is no better feeling than the warm and private glow of satisfaction you get when you reach out to others. And it lasts a lifetime in the knowledge of the hundreds of patients your gift continues to help—perhaps even friends and loved ones—for years to come.

(G) Thank you so much . . . and we look forward to hearing from you very soon.

Sincerely,

Name
Position

(H)

86

Suggested Study Procedure

1. Read the letter straight through at your normal reading pace. Ask yourself, "Good, bad, or somewhere in between?"
2. Re-read the letter slowly.
3. Use the CopyRater™ to evaluate the letter in detail. Add your score. Then note the most important strengths and weaknesses.
4. Compare your ratings with the author's at the back of the workbook.
5. Read the essay at the end of this Study Unit.
6. Write the suggested Exercise material.
7. Review all the work, then add the most important idea(s) to your own developing personal list of letter-writing guidelines.

Exercises

1. Short of rewriting the entire letter, please correct the biggest single weakness you find in this letter.
2. Revise this letter so it only contains Cindy's story. Make the letter more intense.

Comments About This Letter

This two page letter to former patients does a good job of managing a large number of stories, holding reader interest, and constantly reminding the reader that donor generosity plays a direct role in the good outcome of the hospital's patients.

(A) The lead is an intelligent way to get the crucial point in—that the reader is a former patient at the hospital.

Let's talk about leads a bit. The best thing that can happen in a lead is to get over onto the reader's mental side of the street, and "Time has slipped by quickly since you were a patient at Auburndale Hospital" is an elegant way to achieve that.

You might like to take the lead of your last letter and see if you can rewrite it so the reader's particular interests are the main point of the paragraph. (If you've already done that, congratulations!)

With great skill the writer links the reader as a former patient to all the other former patients, ". . . including little Candy Turner."

Off We Go

(B) Here is the second main point of the letter, that some of the Hospital's equipment is purchased as a result of contributor generosity, and many of the contributors are former patients!

(C) The function of the stories is to show how important sophisticated and expensive equipment has been in the care they have received. The stories also demonstrate that the the Hospital is using modern, innovative medical techniques on behalf of its patients.

(D) Here is the ask, and it's a good one. It is extremely well set up.

(E) The size of your gift doesn't matter—your participation at any level, may help save lives. A good point, but I think it would be sensible to include a suggested gift array,

> "Your gift, whether it is $10, $15, $25 or even more, can help us buy . . ."

(F) Reassurance here, too—a composite of three "reasons why" the donor will derive satisfaction from the contribution.

(G) Urging the donor to do it now. This is probably the best thing you can do at the end of the letter, and it would be better still if there were a specific reason why the Hospital wanted an early reply, e.g., "We must make critical decisions about new equipment by the end of this month, so won't you take a moment or two more and write a check right now? We'll appreciate it very much, and your gift will begin to help us save lives just that much sooner."

(H) I miss a P.S. here. As we've said, a P.S. is a high readership point in your letter, which readers are said to skip to in the hope of saving time. If that's true (and one may logically assume that it is), a P.S. should either restate the message, add a new reason to give (the new reason could be a premium) or reinforce the time urgency of a response. A very long P.S. can have a significant positive impact on the "pull" of the letter.

The Letter Overall

This is an extremely skillful letter. It tells stories and touches some, if not all, of the right buttons. But perhaps my use of the word "button" tells you my reservations about the letter.

The warmth seems a little forced and there are too many things going on for maximum effectiveness—too many stories, too many reasons to give at the end. It seems to me a little like a collection of letters.

You can't ask readers to juggle too many balls (or stories) in the air at one time. Perhaps any of the three stories in the letter, told in a little greater detail, would make the point to the satisfaction of the reader?

The multiple stories may also tend to move the letter away from its proper focus—the generosity of the reader and the hospital's need—so that I have a slight feeling the gift idea is being dragged back in here and there.

If you told one story that demonstrated a clear strength of the Hospital, and then you built an equipment need that would help the Hospital do an even better job, you'd have a response that would in all likelihood exceed the one this letter drew.

And what about an offer of recognition? A P.S. that says, "We'll be proud to record your name in our Book of Friends displayed in our lobby" would increase response.

Reading and rereading this letter, I have a slight sense that its elaborate and complex approach may be due partly to a need to impress hospital management, who generally seem to want a fund-raising letter to say everything about the institution and find it hard to understand that a simple, clear letter is generally going to outpull a more spectacular-looking effort. (But it will!)

STUDY UNIT

12

Watch a pro stick to the main point of his letter

(Sample: letter to a major donor)

Dear Friend:

(A) Four times a year, Mrs. Barnett receives a check from the Auburndale Foundation. **(B)**

(C) No, she's not an employee. She's an Annuity Partner—a special friend of ours who enjoys two important benefits: a guaranteed income for life and the satisfaction of helping young people here at the Auburndale Foundation.

(D) I'm sending you this letter today with the prayer that you will join Mrs. Barnett as an Annuity Partner. I want you to enjoy the same special relationships and benefits she does.

(F) But before I tell you how you can become an Annuity Partner, please read how Mrs. Barnett feels about her investment:

(E) "I'm very pleased to be an Annuity Partner. I enjoy a very safe investment, excellent tax benefits, and I receive a guaranteed income for life. But the thing that makes me happiest is knowing I'm able to help the Foundation continue its ministry of training young people for Christian service. Yes, I could have left my money in a savings account to earn interest, but I felt God wanted me to put it to work for him."

(G) You can see how important Mrs. Barnett's investment is to her. That's why I'm confident in asking you to prayerfully consider becoming an Annuity Partner.

In fact, there's never been a better time than now to become an Annuity Partner. Rates for annuities are at an all-time high—ranging from 5.0% to 14%. And, you also receive:

1. A guaranteed income for life
2. Many favorable tax advantages.
3. A safe way to invest your money
4. The ability to pass along the benefits of your investment to anyone that you choose.

Even more important, as an Annuity Partner, you'll have the special feeling of satisfaction knowing you are furthering the gospel.

But how do you know if investing in an Annuity is right for you? We've made it as simple as possible.

(H) Just take the enclosed Inquiry Form and answer each question in full. Then slip the form in the postage-paid envelope and drop it in the mailbox.

(I) And rest assured that the information you provide is confidential and will place you under no obligation.

(J) When we receive your Inquiry Form, we will determine the amount of interest and annual income you would receive from your investment. This information will then be listed on a completed Annuity Application which we will mail you.

After you receive the application, examine it carefully. Then if you feel an Gift Annuity is for you, simply sign the application and return it with your check or money order.

It's a simple way to make an eternal investment in the Lord's work at the Auburndale Foundatin, and to earn a guaranteed income for life.

(K) So please take a moment right now to read the enclosed brochure which answers the most common questions asked about annuities. Then complete the Inquiry Form and drop it in the mail to me today.

(L) I'm eager for you to join special friends like Mrs. Barnett as an Annuity Partner. I look forward to hearing from you.

Sincerely in Christ,

Name
Position

(M) P.S. Let me stress again that completing the Inquiry Form will not place you under any obligation whatsoever. Why not mail it today to determine if an Annuity is right for you? Thank you.

Suggested Study Procedure

1. Read the letter straight through at your normal reading pace. Ask yourself, "Good, bad, or somewhere in between?"
2. Re-read the letter slowly.
3. Use the CopyRater™ to evaluate the letter in detail. Add your score. Then note the most important strengths and weaknesses.
4. Compare your ratings with the author's at the back of the workbook.
5. Read the essay at the end of this Study Unit.
6. Write the suggested Exercise material.
7. Review all the work, then add the most important idea(s) to your own developing personal list of letter-writing guidelines.

Exercises

1. Short of rewriting the entire letter, please correct the biggest single weakness you find in this letter.
2. Write a brief follow-up letter to be mailed a month after this one, restating the same points, but in half the lines. Make it clear this will be the last letter and you need a response!

Comments About This Letter

Let's examine a letter prepared by a pro. Every line is based on the basic rules of selling by mail. I don't have statistics, but am betting it was a big winner.

It is also—see if you agree—far from the way you might write a letter "naturally." Every nuance is jettisoned in favor of simplicity and sell.

> "Four times a year, Mrs. Barnett receives a
> check from the Auburndale Foundation."

(A) That story-telling, money centered, brief lead paragraph would be a good lead for a prospect letter—but it's an even better beginning for a letter to a donor to the Foundation, because the donor already has a strong interest in its work.

(B) Why is it especially good for a donor? It reverses the normal "We are asking you for money and here's why" approach the donor is used to. Few donors would fail to read on!

(C) This paragraph continues the story and follows the classic direct mail sales dictum: hit your most important sales point first.

The benefit, ". . . a guaranteed income for life," is linked to the reason most donors contribute to the Foundation: ". . . the satisfaction of helping young people here . . ." which is also described as a benefit to the donor.

The paragraph is a terrific demonstration of how much meaning you can pack in with concise, well organized and well-punctuated writing.

It also suggests a way in which the donor can upgrade her relationship with the Foundation:

> "She's an Annuity Partner—a special friend of
> ours . . ." (underlining ours)

(D) In this paragraph the donor is offered, prayerfully, the ". . . same special relationship and benefits . . ." Mrs. Barnett enjoys.

(E) It was probably tempting to the copywriter to plunge right on here and complete the invitation. Instead, he or she offered a very reassuring, complete, quote from Mrs. Barnett.

Key points in the quote: (1) It is very direct and says exactly what the Foundation wants said; (2) it moves from telling what a good deal the Annuity Partnership is to ". . . safe investment, excellent tax benefits, and guaranteed income for life." Then it expands on the basic reason most donors contribute and ends with ". . . I felt God wanted me to put it to work for Him."

(F) Here the letter follows a classic direct mail approach—tell the person what she is about to read first and tell her what she just read afterwards. Repeat the key points.

(It would not be a bad exercise for you to go through this letter and see how many actual different points are made and how many ideas are expressed. The number might surprise you on the low side! That's good, and the reason is that it is keeping the reader focused on the argument for becoming an Annuity Partner. Digressions always cost you response and when you can eliminate virtually all digressions, as here, you can count on a strong response.)

(G) Here are the rates paid (what a range)! Then the key points are stressed for the third time, now in a numbered list format.

(H) Note that the Foundation is not asking for a financial commitment. A very official-looking Inquiry Form is part of the package and the donor is invited to fill it in to obtain further information.

Note how exact and simple the instructions are, right down to ''. . . drop it in the mailbox.'' They are followed in the next paragraph by an assurance of confidentiality.

(I) This paragraph is one of the cleverest in the letter. It is designed to arouse the donor's curiosity as to ''. . . the amount of interest and annual income you would receive from your investment.''

(J) This paragraph assures the reader that she is making no commitment at this time, that the decision is still ahead of her. That's another basic of direct mail selling: you are not committing yourself to anything, why not take a look at this?

(K) It makes sense to use a Questions and Answers brochure in this package. Since the commitment is in fact substantial, the more time the donor spends with the mailing the more likely she is to respond.

(L) This paragraph simply reinforces the idea that the prospect should reply now.

(M) The P.S. repeats the ''You aren't committing yourself to anything'' theme—the key point of this letter, whose purpose is to get maximum response from people who can become Annuity Partners if so inclined.

In Conclusion

The more you study this letter, the more you will see that with iron discipline, the writer is throwing out anything that doesn't serve the copy purpose: to get an inquiry. That is instructive. All writing requires discipline, and fund-raising copy, because it is so totally focused on creating a financial response on the part of the reader, requires even more discipline than most forms of writing.

Every fact that isn't needed, every digressive idea, reduces the chance of response just a little bit.

STUDY UNIT

13

Using a story to bring your appeal to life

(Sample: letter from a hospital)

A PRECIOUS BIT OF LIFE . . .

(A) Nicole at 2 1/4 pounds lies in a small intensive care unit in the Newborn Special Care Nursery minutes after her birth.

Nicole's beginning is the story of over 300 premature and critically ill infants cared for last year in this special Nursery.

Sensitive monitors measure her heart rate, blood pressure and temperature. A respirator helps her to breathe. She is fed intravenously and transfusions maintain the delicate balance her body needs. Warming lights keep her body temperature normal.

The Newborn Special Care Nursery at Auburndale Hospital is this state's primary intensive care nursery. Nearly half of all infants come from outside of the city.

Gradually Nicole is able to breathe on her own. She gains weight—a few ounces at a time. Finally, after 11 long weeks, Nicole goes home with her parents.

Many very small infants—some weighing less than two pounds—stay in the Nursery up to 12 weeks. Others are able to go home after 4 or 6 weeks.

Last year an average of 8 babies each day were cared for in this Special Nursery. The average today is 12. More monitors, intensive care beds and respirators are needed to care for these infants . . . to give them the chance they deserve.

(B) Your earlier support helped bring the linear accelerator to the Cancer Therapy Center. As a result, cancer patients in this state are now able to receive advanced radiation therapy treatment without having to travel outside the state. Your gift this Fall will join with many others in providing the best possible care for our very smallest citizens. **(C)**

(D) Voluntary gifts speak of personal concern for others . . . a concern that is both inspiring and encouraging. Your gift will help the next Nicole successfully "graduate" from this Very Special Nursery.

Signed
On behalf of this year's 400 infants

(E) P.S. If you receive a second invitation to help the nursery this fall, please share it with a neighbor. Those who follow Nicole could use the extra help.

Suggested Study Procedure

1. Read the letter straight through at your normal reading pace. Ask yourself, "Good, bad, or somewhere in between?"
2. Re-read the letter slowly.
3. Use the CopyRater™ to evaluate the letter in detail. Add your score. Then note the most important strengths and weaknesses.
4. Compare your ratings with the author's at the back of the workbook.
5. Read the essay at the end of this Study Unit.

6. Write the suggested Exercise material.

7. Review all the work, then add the most important idea(s) to your own developing personal list of letter-writing guidelines.

Exercises

1. Short of rewriting the entire letter, please correct the biggest single weakness you find in this letter.

2. Reorganize the sequence of ideas in this letter so it flows more smoothly—all of the story should be together, for starters.

3. Write a new lead that's still about Nicole, but also starts to make the case for a gift immediately.

Comments About This Letter

This letter ran on two separate sheets, rather than front and back on one sheet. I favor the use of two sheets, because it seems to me to be more like a normal personal letter approach.

A company that has tested front and back versus separate sheets extensively told me that it is satisfied the separate sheets sufficiently outpull front and back printing on one piece of paper to warrant the cost of the extra sheet.

I feel a bit negative about "a precious bit of life. It is eyecatching, which is the point, but it isn't as interesting as the true lead paragraph. It would be good if the eye were directed more strongly to this excellent "story" beginning. Perhaps it could have begun this way:

> "Minutes after Birth"
> "Nicole lies in a tiny intensive care bed in our
> newborn Special Care Nursery. She weighs two
> and a half pounds."

(A) The writer chose to mix two narratives—Nicole's and the story of the Special Nursery—by using italic and roman type.

I think this is confusing to the reader. It's very important in copy to make your story track well so readers don't become confused and lose interest.

Perhaps the letter would have benefitted by beginning with Nicole's story and getting her home safe, then going on to tell how her story is similar to the stories of many other infants in the Newborn Special Care Nursery.

Her story is beautifully told. The details of the nursery are interesting and succinct. They would flow naturally together as a single narrative.

(B) On page two, the indented material would make a marvelous P.S. Where it is now, it interrupts the progression of ideas in the letter.

(C) I want to pay a special tribute to the phrase ". . . Our very smallest citizen . . ." If ever I saw a phrase well-chosen to ring emotional bells with a donor, that's one!

(D) This last paragraph is nice, too, but would be stronger if specific gifts were suggested.

Since this is a letter to donors, I would suggest something like this: "Won't you help our next 'Nicole' graduate from our very Special Nursery? Could you look back at your last generous gift and send an even larger one for this wonderful work? You'll be helping to save infants who need all the help they can get.

That's one alternative in a printed letter. Another would be a paragraph that includes a specific array of gifts from quite high to quite low so as to cover all the donors. Fund-raising letters are always strengthened by specificity in the "ask."

(E) As noted above, I'd love to see the indented material made into a two paragraph P.S. This P. S. I don't like, because it is a negative in a place of high readership. I want a selling point here. If it's necessary to include this point, I would relegate it to the reply slip or reply envelope. Despite the suggestion about giving it to a neighbor (which I have never known to happen), it isn't a reason to give.

The Letter Overall

The letter has a very appealing subject matter, some really fine writing, and an excellent, warm, personal tone. I think its organization could have been better however. The simplest, most logical sequence of paragraphs is always the best one to use.

Thank you, 'Nicole!'

The presence of a real child, with a name, in this letter makes the letter far more memorable for the reader. You could take Nicole out of this letter and still make all the same points about the Special Care Nursery, the need for help, and so on, but they won't be anywhere near as interesting as when you are telling us how a baby named Nicole got saved.

This principle of centering your appeal on a recognizably individual person is so central to effective direct mail fund-raising it should probably be a law: whenever possible, write about people.

STUDY UNIT

14

Writing a fund-raising letter to your peers

(Sample: educational letter for professional fundraising society)

Dear "First Name,"

(A) Are we just going to stand here and take it?

(B) Heck no, we're not! We're going to complete our 1982 Regional Educational Fund appeal this month and we're going to lead the entire country in total participation and total pledges just as we did in 1981.

And do you know why we're going to do it? I'll tell you! We're going to make a gift or pledge to help support the educational program of NAHD because:

If we reach our national goal of $17,500 we will meet the challenge requirement from an interested donor and "earn" another $5,000 gift. Right? Right on!

If we hit the $22,500 grand total goal, we are sure to attract other gifts from grant making foundations, vendors and others.

If we get between 20 and 30 additional gifts and pledges to hit $25,000 or more for our region, we will win a $250.00 prize to be used for a future regional conference and regain our position as "Numero Uno" in the whole country. (I hate to tell you, but Regions V, VI, and X are ahead of us now.)

You want more? Okay!

Voluntary non-profit hospitals need more than ever to reinforce their development efforts with a strong national public awareness effort— and this takes money that we don't get through our regular memberships. We must build up that education fund so it can lead the way in public understanding as well as help achieve our other professional educational goals.

(C) Now, do you know what we are going to do? Sure you do! We are going to sit down right now and we are going to write a check or a pledge (payable before 12/31/82, of course) for $25.00 or more (many have given $50 and $100 gifts, and the average is $57). Twenty-five dollars is the minimum for the competition, but you know that all gifts are welcome.

And then we are going to send it to the National Office so it gets "on the record" before September 30 for credit to our regional goal, in time for the National Conference in October.

If you don't get it in by then, are you off the hook? You know better than that! No—if you don't mail your gift or pledge by September 30, I will personally descend on you at the National Conference in Cincinnati and your gift will still count toward the national competition.

If you don't mail your gift or pledge, and you don't go to the National Conference, are you off the hook? Heh, heh, You knew the answer, didn't you? No, you're not. If you don't mail it by September 30 and don't give at the National Conference, your name goes on my other list. And you know what that means, don't you? Sure you do!

Cordially,

Signer, Chairman
Regional Education Fund

(**D**) P.S. I know we'll all be proud to see our names on the honor roll as national winners in the next issue of NAHD News. Let's go for it.

Suggested Study Procedure

1. Read the letter straight through at your normal reading pace. Ask yourself, "Good, bad, or somewhere in between?"
2. Re-read the letter slowly.
3. Use the CopyRater™ to evaluate the letter in detail. Add your score. Then note the most important strengths and weaknesses.
4. Compare your ratings with the author's at the back of the workbook.
5. Read the essay at the end of this Study Unit.
6. Write the suggested Exercise material.
7. Review all the work, then add the most important idea(s) to your own developing personal list of letter-writing guidelines.

Exercises

1. Short of rewriting the entire letter, please correct the biggest single weakness you find in this letter.
2. Revise this letter so it would go specifically and personally to someone who contributed the previous year. Make him or her know that it is CRUCIAL to renew and to increase their gift.

Comments About This Letter

This letter is entertaining! And it was a winner. One of many such letters sent to National Association of Hospital Development members, state by state, in support of its education fund, this one drew record dollars and a record percentage of response.

It is a peer-to-peer letter and that dictates the tone, the humor, and the wonderfully relentless "ask."

(I would break any fund-raising letter into five elements and rank those elements in this exact order: who's being asked; what's being asked; how is the ask being put; how much is being asked for; and who's asking. In this case, though, who's asking is much more important than usual.)

If someone read this who had no commitment to or association with the NAHD, he or she would be extremely unlikely to respond. That's important to remember, because the more you "slant" your copy to what you know about your reader, the better your response is likely to be.

The author of this letter knows many, perhaps most, of the people on the list. He feels free to take an imaginative approach, to be enthusiastic, to be funny, and to hit his key points hard and often.

(A) The lead is excellent. "Are we just going to stand here and take it?" Who wouldn't read on? Take what?

(B) In the second paragraph, the author works in a "we" that for once is an obvious "you and me" rather than a distant "we" that obviously doesn't include the reader.

Then he follows up with a firm, confident, entirely up-beat promise in paragraph two. People LOVE optimism and enthusiasm (and will respond to it)!

Next he says how the promise will be kept. He uses bullets in the one way that makes sense to me—to organize and simplify a number of complicated ideas. In a few lines he tells about a challenge gift, the need to reach to total, and a prize that will make "our" region "Numero Uno." In a strong parenthesis, he tells the reader 3 other regions are still ahead.

Lots of strong "band wagon" psychology going on in this letter! The band wagon idea, too, is something that people respond to.

(C) Next (this part I like even more than the first part) he spends the rest of the letter, nearly half, talking about:

HOW MUCH

HOW TO SEND YOUR GIFT

WHY YOU SHOULD SEND IT NOW

HOW RELENTLESS MY FOLLOW UP WILL BE

Which culminates in a delicious and only mock-humorous threat to put the reader on my other list.

(D) He then uses a P.S. to promise recognition—a very sound additional "reason to give."

We learn from the best letters, the ones that read well and demonstrate pulling power. This is an excellent letter to study and emulate. But I would like to tack on a few cautions and suggestions here.

The first is that this technique, so effective with a member of the same profession, would not work unless there were a strong tie between the organization and the individual. That's a must.

The second is that humor is generally not effective in fund-raising. One reason I like this letter so well is that it is an extremely rare bird—a funny letter that makes a serious case. People just don't seem to like humor about their money. So be careful.

The third is that the author has spent much of his letter talking about the donor's gift. In my experience, the more you focus on that gift, which is your true subject, the higher the response will be.

And the final thought is that I wish, since the letter is addressed by name, that it would have been possible to have two slightly different versions: one addressed to donors in other years exhorting them to increase the level of their giving by a reasonable (and specific) amount; the second reading pretty much as here.

You do have two different audiences out there: those who have given, and those who haven't. If you recognize that different status in your copy, your results will improve. And the better you do it, the better a yield you will have from each mailing.

STUDY UNIT

15

Best way to keep a donor in the "active" file

(Sample: thank you letter to donor)

Dear Friend:

(A) Thank you for your pledge to purchase this special children's ticket. Your generosity has enabled many worthy local children to attend this special performance of "THE INTERNATIONAL ALL STAR CIRCUS."

(B) Enclosed you will find a perforated ticket. One side is the Sponsorship Pass for the children to attend—the other is your family ticket. Please sign your Sponsorship Pass and return it, along with your check, for distribution so the handicapped and worthy children may attend with your compliments.

(C) If, for some reason, you are unable to attend the show, you may give your family ticket to relatives or friends, or return it to us and that would allow that many more children to attend in your name. In the event these tickets are not used, they will be considered a donation.

(D) As you know, it takes much time and advance preparation to get the transportation and arrangements made for the children to see the show, so won't you please help us to help these children in dropping your Sponsorship Pass and check in the mail today? We have enclosed a return envelope for your convenience.

Because of people like you, we will be able to keep our commitments, and bring joy to the many deserving citizens in this area. We are sure that you and your family will enjoy this 90 minute entertainment show that features Animal Acts, Illusions, Magical Acts, Acts of Daring, and an Old Time Brass Band. This is a professional circus that performs in over 200 cities and towns each year.

If you have any further questions, or would like to purchase additional tickets, please feel free to call.

Many thanks,

Signer
Position

Suggested Study Procedure

1. Read the letter straight through at your normal reading pace. Ask yourself, "Good, bad, or somewhere in between?"
2. Re-read the letter slowly.
3. Use the CopyRater™ to evaluate the letter in detail. Add your score. Then note the most important strengths and weaknesses.
4. Compare your ratings with the author's at the back of the workbook.
5. Read the essay at the end of this Study Unit.
6. Write the suggested Exercise material.
7. Review all the work, then add the most important idea(s) to your own developing personal list of letter-writing guidelines.

Exercises

1. Short of rewriting the entire letter, please correct the biggest single weakness you find in this letter.

2. Find a way, without reducing the effectiveness of the thank you, to persuade the donor to buy more tickets.

Comments About This Letter

A hot weeknight in July between 7 and 8 p.m. I had a hard day and a full meal and am starting to moulder when the phone rings.

"Hi, this is the Kiwanis Club," a girl's voice says. "You remember last year you bought some tickets to our circus for some handicapped children?"

"Yes," I say guardedly.

"How many would you like this year?"

Oh mercy, I think. I don't need this!

"How many did I get last year?" I ask. "Three," she says.

"Well, put me down for three this year."

End of conversation. There go some more bucks, I think. Two days later I got the Kiwanis mailing—a nice-looking ticket that said ADMIT THREE on it, a reply envelope, and the letter you see. I was about to pass it along for payment but stopped to read the letter.

By the end of it I felt good about what I was doing! I wasn't just forking over 12 bucks to Kiwanis, I was sending children to the circus.

The thing I feel is most important in direct mail fund-raising—making the donor feel good about what he or she is accomplishing—this letter did for me.

Let's see WHY this letter works so well. The first thing I notice is that it is a very busy letter—there is a great deal to be said and not much space.

(By "needs to be said" I don't mean long explanations of how great the circus is or what a difficult time handicapped children have or what a fine organization Kiwanis is.

I mean "thank you—here's your ticket—here's how it works—please hurry—here's what you will be doing—if you have questions or would like to buy more tickets, call." All these points have to be covered.)

As a result, the letter has a brisk tone—a good thing to strive for in any fund-raising letter. I've noticed for years that the faster a letter appears to read, the better it seems to do. (I don't mean a short letter, a long letter can just as easily be fast reading.)

(A) In Paragraph One, we're thanked, reminded that we made a "pledge," and told specifically what will happen as a result of our generosity. It could hardly be more succinct.

(B) Paragraph Two explains the (necessarily) complicated double ticket that accompanies the letter. One half of it is a group ticket admitting three kids, one half is a ticket for three for the contributor.

You are told just what to do with the two tickets and given the option of sending your own tickets back so more kids can go—a chance to do even more good.

(C) Paragraph Three gives you a good, believable reason to send the money now—the time and preparation required to get the trip organized.

(D) Paragraph Four tells you again, in specific terms, what a nice thing you're doing. And the final paragraph offers a chance to send more money.

Nobody would say this is a moving letter, or elegant, or even well written (not that it is badly written). It draws no attention to itself.

But that is often—almost always, really—the nature of an effective direct mail letter. It is all function and not much form. It is about the reader and the need and not about being "a nice piece of writing."

And this one did get the job done effectively. It is exceptionally specific about the things it needs to be specific about—what the donor is actually going to do. And its focus is the donor.

Possible Improvements

I can't think of a thing I'd change in this letter other than to try a personalized version as a test and see if the considerable extra cost would be justified by increased pull. In this case, I doubt it.

But the Kiwanis could improve the campaign in two ways: one, in the weeks just before the phoning gets under way, mail a letter to all donors thanking them for their commitment, telling them a call will be coming "in the near future," and expressing the hope they will be even more generous this year; two, during the call, have the solicitor say, "Mr. Squires, last year you were kind enough to sponsor three children for $12.00. Would you consider sponsoring six kids this year?"

Pre-call letters have demonstrated an ability to increase the renewal rates of the calls and to set up successful upgrading requests.

I do think that since the "ask" is to send handicapped children to the circus, it's sensible and easy, really, for phoners to ask for an upgrade. Especially if a letter plants that idea before the call is made.

In Conclusion

This letter is an especially good example of the value of making the donor the star of every transaction. When you sit down to write a fund-raising letter, you always have some pressure to make your institution the star, and there is a natural tendency to want to get people to say "What a good letter!" But both those things really must take a back seat to the need to make the donor the star for a mailing to be successful.

16

Dramatizing the day-to-day work

(Sample: Heart Care Center letter for a hospital)

Mr. David A. Sample
Apartment 22
22 Sample Street
Auburndale, MA 02166

Dear Mr. Sample:

(A) Suddenly, David Harris felt like an elephant was standing on his chest!

(B) "I knew I would die if I denied I was having a heart attack," he said. David was rushed to our Heart Care Center where specialists detected the complete blockage of a major coronary artery.

(C) Within moments, the decision was made to administer a revolutionary new drug called "streptokinase." David watched on a monitor as a thin tube was threaded through his arteries to the blockage and the drug injected into his clot.

"It was thrilling," relates David. "Quickly the clot dissolved and the blood shot through my artery!"

(C) Amazingly, what David Harris witnessed was his heart attack being stopped BEFORE it could run its course.

(D) Today David is at home with his family—thankful for the life-saving treatment he received at Auburndale Hospital. Personally, I feel all of us should be thankful our hospital offers such "state-of-the-art" health care.

(E) But it doesn't happen automatically. In order for Auburndale Hospital to maintain this margin of excellence, we depend on the generosity of caring citizens—former patients like you. Please, send a gift of $20, $25, or $30 to keep Auburndale Hospital strong. When you do—we all benefit!

Gratefully yours,
Name
Position

(F) P.S. With the beginning of the new year, this is a good time to make a generous, tax-deductible gift. Thank you.

Suggested Study Procedure

1. Read the letter straight through at your normal reading pace. Ask yourself, "Good, bad, or somewhere in between?"
2. Re-read the letter slowly.
3. Use the CopyRater™ to evaluate the letter in detail. Add your score. Then note the most important strengths and weaknesses.
4. Compare your ratings with the author's at the back of the workbook.
5. Read the essay at the end of this Study Unit.
6. Write the suggested Exercise material.
7. Review all the work, then add the most important idea(s) to your own developing personal list of letter-writing guidelines.

Exercises

1. Short of rewriting the entire letter, please correct the biggest single weakness you find in this letter.

114

2. Add two paragraphs to show that David Harris did not have a unique experience. Show how this kind of medicine benefits the reader and his or her family.

3. Replace the "ask" paragraph with one at least twice as strong and specific.

Comments About This Letter

Here is a hard-working letter to prospects. The copy is excellent and the format is worth discussing, too.

(A) Nice lead! It has high energy, it is very personal, it reads quickly, and it is all too credible.

(B) The quote is good. I believe that people are more attentive to quotes than other writing.

The quote reflects the denial phenomenon often associated with heart attacks. It is an odd thing for David Harris to say, but its oddness contributes to its interest.

After the quote the paragraph moves fast—perhaps a shade too fast for easy reading. You might lose readers with the second sentence.

(C) Paragraph Three and Four are sensational! They hold your interest just as all good medical writing does.

These two paragraphs show the Hospital at its best. No reader would ask for better proof of the Hospital's ability to save a life.

(D) I think the letter weakens in this paragraph. It is important to the case to be able to say "David is at home with his family." But the rest of the sentence and the one that follows it don't add to the case for a gift—especially "Personally, I feel all of us should be thankful . . . ," which I think readers will ignore.

(E) In this paragraph, the "it" is a problem. It refers to "state-of-the-art health care," but that is a hard connection to make.

The following sentence, with its somewhat cliched "margin of excellence," is just not a real reason to give.

The last two sentences, from "Please . . ." on, are direct and succinct—good stuff.

The gift range in this paragraph "$20, $25, or $30—is too high to get a maximum number of responses.

It's better to ask for $10 and get as many first-time gifts as possible. Upgrading can take place later.

(F) The P.S. is weak, I feel. The idea that a new year has begun is not in itself a persuasive reason to give. If you are going to make a point you must make it strongly.

115

This letter is excellent for its excitement, personal approach, choice of story and method of telling it.

But it seems likely that its pull might have been increased significantly by tying the gift request in the last two paragraphs to the cost of such magnificent care.

The cost in research, the cost in equipment, the cost in skilled personnel, are all good "reasons why" we ask former patients at the Hospital for financial support.

Another response strengthener might have been to direct the appeal to a specific piece of heart-related equipment.

I am sure this letter did well, though. The underlying message—your contribution to this hospital helps us protect you against such things as heart attacks—would be clear to any reader, and especially to a recent former patient, now recovering!

This was a classic "carbon" of a computer letter, although of course it does not show up as such here. It was printed as the second part of a computer form, with a sheet of carbon paper behind the impacted original. (The computer happily shuttled back and forth between its list of names and addresses of former patients and its satellite printer, merging names with text.)

The two-part form (it could have been a three part form with an original and two carbons) was burst, trimmed, and inserted into envelopes. The original letters were mailed out. Then responses were checked against the carbons and the carbons were mailed to all who have not yet responded.

A printed "handwritten" note exhorts the prospect to give and to cover the possibility of a gift and an appeal letter crossing in the mail. The note is printed as part of the form.

This format is cost-effective because you get two (or three) letters in a single printing. Whatever the response to the original was, the response to the carbon is likely to be about half. This means that if you had a strong pull from your original, you'll do well with the carbon. Unfortunately, if your original was a dud, the carbon will be a double dud!

STUDY UNIT
17
Using memorable details to make your appeal hit home

(Sample: letter to donors from a Catholic mission in the American Southwest)

(A) (date goes here)

Dear Friend,

(B) Happy 1982! May our loving Lord grant you all the special blessings you hope for in this new year!

(C) We came into the new year in debt. Thanks to you and other wonderful friends I have been able to pay the biggest bills (like insurance for the church, buses, etc.).

(D) Now that these bills are paid, we are broke again. Yet I know that God will continue to use this time of testing to bestow many blessings.

I believe that God wants to see how strong our faith is, and how strongly we want to serve our

Indian brothers and sisters. When we come through this hard time, the hope of a good school for our Indian boys and girls will become a reality!

(E) Even as we went broke, it seemed more families in need came for help. One Sunday, nine people were stranded from car accidents on the icy roads. One young Indian girl had to be rushed to the hospital thirty miles away to get stitches for the deep cuts on her face.

We fed the people with our soup and sandwiches, and I know how grateful they were to find warmth and concern here in "the middle of nowhere."

Shirley Largo came by two days ago to tell me of a mother with five children and severe personal and family problems. No clothes, no water, no transportation! The various government programs could not help! So we had some clothes, some food, and I am trying to get a fifty gallon sanitary drum for their water (they only have a ten gallon can).

You would be filled with happiness for the next month if you could see the look of relief and elation on that mother's face!

(F) There are many others suffering who we could help if we had more funds. Meanwhile, we carry on everything we can. Our religious education classes are filled with Navajo boys and girls. One day God will call some of them to be priests and sisters and they will be able to care for this mission!

We count on your prayers every day. Your prayers and ours will get all the blessings we need to keep serving the Lord and His poor Indians here.

If you can send a donation, it will be greatly appreciated and do a lot of good. God will see that your generosity to His works will be rewarded ten times over. I keep the slips of paper with your special intentions on the altar as I pray for you every day at Holy Mass.

God bless you!

In Jesus' Loving Heart,

Name

(H) P.S. Thanks to you, we were able to rush the young Indian girl to the hospital. Your donations paid the insurance for our truck this month.

Suggested Study Procedure

1. Read the letter straight through at your normal reading pace. Ask yourself, "Good, bad, or somewhere in between?"
2. Re-read the letter slowly.
3. Use the CopyRater™ to evaluate the letter in detail. Add your score. Then note the most important strengths and weaknesses.
4. Compare your ratings with the author's at the back of the workbook.
5. Read the essay at the end of this Study Unit.
6. Write the suggested Exercise material.
7. Review all the work, then add the most important idea(s) to your own developing personal list of letter-writing guidelines.

Exercises

1. Short of rewriting the entire letter, please correct the biggest single weakness you find in this letter.
2. Write a letter for a nonsectarian children's home (25–30 lines) that would have the same kind of realism this letter does. Invent the details.
3. Slant the letter to someone who has contributed but not in the past year—a lapsed donor. Try VERY hard for a renewal.

Comments About This Letter

You may not be, like the author of this letter, a Catholic priest struggling to keep a small Southwestern mission from going broke.

But I'd like to suggest that you study his letter very carefully, anyway. It is one of the better fund-raising letters to come my way.

Let me also suggest that you put yourself in the frame of mind of the person to whom that letter is addressed: a devout religious person, almost certainly fairly poor, who contributes many times a year to the mission, normally with gifts of less than $10. You are very apt to send specific prayer requests with your gifts.

Here, as I think you will see, is a masterful example of someone who knows his audience so well he is one with them. So even if you might not agree with his approach personally, remember that his donors do!

(A) Starting at the top, every direct mail fund-raising pro I know, me included, feels that if you can put a specific date on your letter, you should. The reason is that the date makes your letter more like a personal letter from one person to one person, which is always the aim in a fund-raising letter.

(B) This is a good lead because it is exactly what the donor would expect to receive from the Father, whom he thinks of on a first-name basis—Father Bill, Father Pete, et cetera.

Most leads, especially to your donors, should begin with the most simple, obvious thing you can think of. They should be very short, as here, and very easy to read—so easy, in fact, that the reader should be able to enter your letter without being conscious of the fact that he or she has started to "study" something. Make it easy.

The second thing that is good about this lead is that it is about the reader, not the institution. If you can think of a way to do that for your organization, you will have much more interested readers than if you start off with your problems and needs.

(C) Here the writer continues the strong "you" orientation by praising the donor for helping the mission accomplish very specific things.

Note the many specific, concrete examples the writer offers in his letter. Every paragraph is made more real by the use of homely, specific details—a crucial ingredient of effective fund-raising communications. Always choose specifics over generalities!

To see the magic of this letter up close, underline every concrete example. Taken together, they give the letter a foundation of authenicity and credibility that is absolutely unquestionable.

The great thing about being specific is that it makes it much easier for people who are reading your letters to see what is happening at your end. Word pictures are memorable!

Note, too, that all the specifics presented in the letter are people-related. Without people, and what happens to them as a result of donor generosity, fund-raising letters are extremely apt to be weak.

(D) In this paragraph, the father begins his "ask," and really never stops appealing thereafter.

Note the simplicity and humility of "we are broke again." Very seldom do organizations wish to reveal to donors that they are less than totally successful at whatever it is they wish to accomplish.

Part of the reason for this, I think, is institutional vanity, but another part is the idea that donors will desert you if they know you have warts in unbecoming places. That's not so. Donors know they are human and therefore imperfect so they also know you are human and therefore imperfect.

So if you show your donors, in concrete terms, the two steps forward, they will forgive you the occasional step back.

I have never seen an organizations's direct mail response diminish as a result of taking its donors into its confidence.

(Besides that, an Indian mission should be broke. It's supposed to be giving away all the money, using all the money, it gets. Many social service organizations that are grass roots and work close to the bone should be operating on a shoestring level—that shows a donor the money is out there doing things for people. So the "we are broke again" is not read by donors as mismanagement, really, but as proof of doing a good job.)

Note, too, in this paragraph, the "dream"—"the hope of a good school for our Indian boys and girls . . ."

(E) From "car accidents on icy roads" to "deep cuts" to "soup and sandwiches" to "Shirley Largo came by" to "a fifty gallon sanitary drum," these three paragraphs are wonderful in their personal detail. I've seldom seen better, more compelling, examples of a human voice in a letter.

Note, too, please, the "You would be filled with happiness for the next month . . ." This is a superb example of sharing the satisfaction of your work with a donor.

(F) The remaining paragraphs add reasons to give—the possibility that the mission will be able to recruit more priests and sisters—the need for, and efficacy of, prayer—and the reminder (again, wonderfully concrete, "I keep the slips of paper with your special intentions by the altar") that the priest will pray for the donor. For the audience, these are powerful reasons to give.

(G) This P.S. is excellent! I am in awe of it. The more you think about its implications to the person who has given to the mission recently, the more powerful it becomes.

Possible Improvements

Anything can be made better. I think the pulling power of this letter would be substantially greater if it could be personalized by name to each donor, and if the donor's last gift date and amount could be mentioned, together with a request for a specific, reasonable gift increase.

I would also like to see price tags put on some of the specific things mentioned. What was the insurance cost for the truck? How much does a fifty gallon drum cost? What did the mission spend to provide soup and sandwiches? And so on. Real cash amounts would tend to produce more response.

How can you apply all this good stuff?

This letter shows how simple good fund-raising copy can be, and often is. The man who wrote it is just working with what is in his heart. He loves what he is doing, he loves the people he is working with, and he loves the donors. And he just lets it all show—he shares what's going on. Any of us can do that, if we believe in what we're doing, know what we're doing, and are willing to share the credit with donors. Good fund-raising copy comes from the heart.

In specifics, try for a modest, human, person-to-person tone. Keep the reader's interests uppermost in your mind. Share the credit for everything with donor. Be concrete. Use frequent examples. Talk about real people. Do these things and it's hard to imagine not getting a good response—I don't think I've ever read a letter that was written with these things uppermost in the writer's mind that didn't do well.

STUDY UNIT
18
Using a good parallel story, or parable

(Sample: letter to donors to a religious camp)

(A) TEAMWORK CAN GET THINGS DONE

(B) When I was Camp Auburndale's director, one of the maintenance workers half buried a tractor in the swamp. The maintenance crew spent two or three days trying to get that tractor out. They even hooked another tractor to it. But nothing worked.

(C) I told the properties director that if he would tie a rope to the tractor, I thought our campers could pull it out of the swamp. I think he was a bit skeptical, but he was out of ideas, so he agreed to try it.

(D) When we arrived to pull it out later that morning, the maintenance crew was gone for coffee. Rather than leave the kids unoccupied, we all got on the rope and began to tug. The maintenance crew got back from their break just in time to watch that tractor being pulled from the swamp!

(E) Right now Camp Auburndale has another "tractor" stuck in the swamp. But this time the "tractor" is our potential and the "swamp" is our debt.

(F) We have a balanced budget projected for this year, but we're still stuck with our debt. We believe we can operate debt free in the future, but we are going to have to find an extra pull to get us out of this hole. **(G)**

Recently one of our staff gave Camp Auburndale $10,000. This money came from many years of personal savings. In fact, this year at least three of our staff families are each giving through volunteer work and special gifts well over $10,000 to Camp Auburndale. These folks are sacrificing because they want Camp Auburndale to provide Bible education for the next generation. **(H)**

(I) We are willing to give; we are willing to work hard, but we can't do it alone. That is where you come in. Would you be willing to give a one-time "Retire the Debt" gift **(J)** to add to what these staff members are giving? Will you give $100 to help Camp Auburndale lay a solid "no debt" foundation again?

(K) If we will each get on the rope and tug just a little, Camp Auburndale can be debt free. Remember, your contribution (of whatever size) will make a difference because we will all be pulling together. I look forward to the celebration when this is done.

(L) Building for the future,

Name
Position

(M) P.S. Some friends of Camp Auburndale recently sent us a check for $1,000 earmarked "for debt retirement". We very much appreciate this family's vision. Perhaps you are one whom God has especially blessed and could also give $1,000 **(N)** or more.

Suggested Study Procedure

1. Read the letter straight through at your normal reading pace. Ask yourself, "Good, bad, or somewhere in between?"
2. Re-read the letter slowly.
3. Use the CopyRater™ to evaluate the letter in detail. Add your score. Then note the most important strengths and weaknesses.
4. Compare your ratings with the author's at the back of the workbook.
5. Read the essay at the end of this Study Unit.
6. Write the suggested Exercise material.
7. Review all the work, then add the most important idea(s) to your own developing personal list of letter-writing guidelines.

Exercises

1. Short of rewriting the entire letter, please correct the biggest single weakness you find in this letter.
2. Use same last half of this letter, but create a completely different story that also gets across the teamwork idea.

Comments About This Letter

I think of this as the "good analogy" letter because the writer used a memorable, believable, and interesting story to give life and excitement to his appeal.

Nothing about this letter was routine. It was printed in brown ink on an orange background, with a good cartoon in white at the top and one at the bottom illustrating, respectively, teamwork and triumph.

(A) Next, instead of an ordinary "dear Friend" or "I am writing to you because I need your help immediately" or some other textbook lead, the writer set this headline in bold type.

I like it because it's simple, direct, and a clear signal of a story to be told. It's also the essential theme of the whole message.

(B) Excellent first paragraph—tight, easy to understand, a good problem to solve, interesting!

(C) "Our campers?" I'm skeptical, too. But curious! Aren't you?

(D) Happy ending! And an essential point for the letter—by working together, the kids were able to do something even another tractor couldn't do!

(E) Here's the bridge paragraph between the story/analogy and the need at hand. The matchup is simple and perfect. Read this paragraph two

125

or three times and I think you'll be more and more impressed by its artful simplicity.

The paragraph brings the organization's "potential" to life and makes the reader understand exactly how hard it is to get things done with a "swamp" of debt to deal with.

This letter could have started right here, with a "Dear Friend." All the key data relevant to the debt and the campaign follows from here on.

But wouldn't something really important have been lost without the tractor story? It was more than a story, it was a parable. And it reminded me just a bit of Pilgrim's Progress.

Parables have always been the best way to help people understand complex concepts—to overcome doubts—to get in synch with one another and cooperate. Yet we rarely see them in fundraising letters! I wonder why.

(F) Here's a statement of a responsible approach by the internal staff. We will not exceed our means again. But that doesn't help us get out of the debt hole.

(G) Well, how are we going to find an extra pull (I like the informality of this language, indeed I like the comfortable, low-key tone of this letter throughout) to get us out of this hole?

Donors like to look and see who's taking the first step. If I have a challenge grant to offer, or if I can cite a big first gift from someone, I know I'm on good ground with donors to a cause because such things (I opine!) relieve the ever-present worry any donor has: Am I doing the right thing here, or should I do something else with my money?

It's a big plus to say that someone else has made big investment in solving the problem—especially someone closely connected to your organization.

There are times when you want to really hit your main theme hard, say it at the beginning, in the middle, and at the end. And there are times when you want to state your theme in another way, as in this letter.

(H) The core "reason to give" of the letter, providing Bible education at the camp for the is given a good specific context. The writer isn't just saying it, he's showing you some people felt so strongly they have put thousands of dollars behind it.

(I) Here's a major flaw in the letter. I don't like the "We are willing to give; we are willing to work hard, but we can't do it alone." This thought is a digression and the ego in it doesn't serve the "ask" at all well. I don't think anybody ever gave a dime because somebody else was working hard, do you?

(J) I also have a reservation about using the phrase "one-time" in any fund-raising letter, even if the organization truly does mean "one time." Surely "a special gift" would do as well and it doesn't leave the unhappy (for the organization) echo in the donor's mind that this will be the last time her or she is solicited. Otherwise, this is an excellent paragraph even the $100 ask, in context, is not too much. And that is a solid achievement.

(K) The final paragraph properly revisits the analogy-parable-metaphor and makes the point that with all of us pulling together, a gift of any size will make a difference. Then it ends on the kind of positive note I love to see in letters. "I look forward to the celebration we'll have when this is done." People like enthusiasm!

(L) I would use "Sincerely yours" because "Building for the future" undercuts the "I look forward to . . ." line a bit.

(M) This P.S. is strong. It is a functional P.S. in that it adds news, and suggests that an even larger gift would be welcome if such is possible. But including it, the writer opened the possibility that some large gifts would come. And they did.

(N) The last line might better ready "$500, $1000 or more," though. The jump from $100 to $1000 is far too big for donors.

It appears to suggest that "You can give $100 or $1000, but nothing in between." That's the way donors would read it.

In Conclusion

What might have improved this very strong, very successful letter? I think an offer of permanent recognition of some sort would have been appropriate to the appeal and successful.

Also, remembering a hugely successful Jerry Falwell "Retire the debt on Liberty Mountain" campaign a few years ago, I wonder whether a "Must Be Done By" approach, giving a date by which the debt absolutely must be paid off, would not have given the letter more urgency and thereby increased response considerably.

The letter deserves high marks on most points, though. It shows that real creativity in direct mail is free—anybody can have a good idea, any time, and folks, I never met an idea in direct mail, meaning a fresh way to make a case, that didn't turn out to be a good idea when the response came back.

STUDY UNIT

19

A great story makes a great letter

(Sample: appeal to prospects on behalf of a hospice)

(A) (date goes here)

(B) "YOUR MOTHER IS VERY, VERY SICK. SHE IS GOING TO DIE. SHE IS NOT GOING TO GET ANY BETTER . . ."

Dear Friend:

(C) As Beverly left her home in early March 1981, she knew she would never return. This would be her final stay in the hospital. Beverly, at age 32, had cancer.

(C) Beverly Rector and her husband, David, an executive with an Auburndale bank, knew this time would come. They had been preparing themselves since early January when Beverly began receiving care from the Auburndale Hospice team. The hardest part had been trying to prepare two young children, Melissa, age 8, and Brian, age 5, for what was to come.

(C) A few years earlier Beverly developed breast cancer and had a mastectomy. She was undergoing reconstructive surgery when a cough developed. Tests showed that cancer had spread to her lungs.

(D) On January 7, 1981, Beverly Fraker Rector was admitted to the Hospice Program.

(E) Hospice is a fairly new idea, but a concept dating to medieval times when people spoke of death surrounded by family and friends as "The Good Death." In the Middle Ages, a hospice was a waystation for weary travelers. Today, Hospice incorporates both concepts. A hospice to prepare individuals and family for "The Good Death" in a comfortable and familiar environment became a reality in Auburndale a few years ago when the hospital introduced the first Hospice Program in the state.

(F) In January, Beverly received chemotherapy at Fort Sanders. When she went home, the Hospice team helped get a hospital bed and other necessary equipment to ensure that she would be comfortable and pain-free as possible.

By late January, Beverly was at home and able to take care of herself and her family. Friends and other family members helped out by bringing in meals and helping with the household. The hospice nurses checked in often. Life was fairly normal.

In mid-February, Beverly was readmitted to Auburndale with breathing problems and had to go on oxygen. She felt weak and was withdrawn. It was during this stay in the hospital that Beverly, with the support of her family and the Hospice team, came to terms with her own death, quietly and privately.

She improved and again went home but now needed around-the-clock care, which was provided by her husband and her mother with assistance from Hospice nurses Nancy Kerr and Beth Santella.

Through the encouragement of the Hospice team, Beverly and David's concerns were verbalized and discussed. The children needed to be prepared, and Beverly was concerned with leaving Melissa and Brian.

Also heavy on her mind was that her children might someday have another mother. This was perhaps the most difficult reality for her to accept. But, again privately working this out, she later expressed her confidence that whomever David might select as a future wife would be good to her children. God had helped her while growing up, she said, and she knew that he would help her children too.

David and Beverly, along with the Hospice nurses, tried to keep family life as normal as possible and involve Melissa and Brian in their mother's care. Melissa would help by tearing tape when Beverly needed an I.V., and Brian would pat her hand, fluff her pillow and do whatever he could. The children were able to give and receive comfort. Often they would climb up in bed and play games or put on a show. Just spending time together was important.

Nancy and Beth were able to control the symptoms and pain so Beverly could enjoy her time at home with her family. She often expressed her desire to be able to die in her sleep, easily, and quietly.

In a few weeks Beverly began to get worse. She asked to go back to Auburndale Hospital.

On March 6, 7 and 8, David and Hospice nurse, Beth Santella, had many conversations about how to prepare the children, and to tell them that death was permanent—their mother was not coming home from the hospital this time. They discussed his feelings about what the children should know, his new role in the family, and the changes that would take place in his life.

David brought Melissa and Brian to the Hospital and, in a secluded conference room, told them, "You know, your mother is very, very sick. She is going to die. She is not going to get any better. She is going to die." Their conversation continued for many minutes, David answering their questions. He then asked if they would like to see their mother.

As Melissa came into the room, she patted Beverly's hand, went to the window, climbed on a chair, and stared out. David took little Brian downstairs. Beverly looked at Melissa and asked, "Do you want to lie down with me?" "Yes, Mommy," she replied. As they lay looking at each other, Melissa asked, "You're not going to get any better, are you?" "No, but I'm okay right now."

On March 13, 1981, Beverly's mother and David were asleep by her bedside. In the predawn hours of the morning, Beverly Fraker Rector quietly and peacefully died, as she had wanted, having come to terms with death.

Although David had prepared himself for this moment, the most difficult time of Beverly's illness came when he had to tell his two children that their mother had died.

(G) Several weeks after the funeral, a letter was discovered in the overnight bag that Beverly always kept packed ready for the Hospital. It was her "goodbye" letter to her husband, her children, and her family.

The letter continued by saying how much she loved and was proud of Melissa and Brian. She expressed her feelings and anticipated theirs.

For some, the realization of death comes hard; for others, it never comes. But all working with the Hospice team know there are people who care, who are concerned, who will listen, and who can be depended upon.

The story of Beverly, David, Melissa and Brian Rector is just one of the hundreds of cases that Nancy and Beth have worked on over the years. No two are ever the same.

Please join us in our efforts to continue to provide this vital and unique service to those individuals who have such a desperate need by sending your tax deductible gift to the Auburndale Hospital Foundation today.

(H) Hospice deals with death, but it is as big as life, helping ensure that as many terminally ill people as possible will live the remainder of their lives, pain free and as normally and happily as possible. **(I)** Auburndale Hospital provides the Hospice Program to the community without charge!

Your gift of $1,000, $500, $100, $20 or even $10 can help assure that this program will be able to continue, expand, and provide this loving care to all who need it.

In this joyous Holiday season think of the many people who are spending this Christmas without their loved ones or who know that they may be spending next Christmas alone.

(J) You can help ease pain and bring comfort to others. Use the enclosed, postage-paid envelope to mail your gift today.

Thank you and may you have a very joyous and happy Holiday season.

Sincerely,

Name
Position

P.S. Please mark the appropriate box on the enclosed envelope to designate your gift to the Auburndale Hospice Program or to the Auburndale Cancer Center.

Suggested Study Procedure

1. Read the letter straight through at your normal reading pace. Ask yourself, "Good, bad, or somewhere in between?"
2. Re-read the letter slowly.
3. Use the CopyRater™ to evaluate the letter in detail. Add your score. Then note the most important strengths and weaknesses.
4. Compare your ratings with the author's at the back of the workbook.
5. Read the essay at the end of this Study Unit.
6. Write the suggested Exercise material.
7. Review all the work, then add the most important idea(s) to your own developing personal list of letter-writing guidelines.

Exercises

1. Short of rewriting the entire letter, please correct the biggest single weakness you find in this letter.
2. In last part of this letter, make more of the reader's possible role. Get more "you" into this letter.

Comments About This Letter

(A) The presence of the date here makes the letter real as a letter even though the next thing, the headline, is unletterlike.

(B) This headline does two things. It tells the reader that a fundamental human drama, a family drama, will be told in the letter, and it draws the reader in brilliantly because everyone can empathize with the situation. A universal bond has been established, a story promised.

(C) In these first three paragraphs, the story, told simply and in detail, begins to unfold. Not a word is wasted. We meet Beverly Rector, her husband David, and their children, Melissa, 8, and Brian, 5. We learn that she faces her second, undoubtedly fatal, bout with cancer that has ". . . spread to her lungs."

(D) We learn that "On January 7, 1981 (the precise day), Beverly Franker Rector (an astonishingly sensitive and good place for the writer to include her maiden name as well as her married name) was admitted to the Auburndale Hospice Program.

(E) It's usually best to eliminate a digression in the middle of a story, but here it is vital that the reader understand the Hospice concept and how it fits in at Auburndale. We don't need concrete details on what the Auburndale Hospice does for people because we'll get that in the rest of the letter, but we need the background.

In a simple, masterful paragraph, the writer reviews the historic hospice concept and tells that it became a reality in Auburndale a few years ago . . ." (Note the gentle one-upmanship of "became a reality in Auburndale" and the refusal to let the reader get bogged down in an unnecessary fact in the phrase "a few years ago.") One of the amazing things about this letter is the writer's consistent ability to choose and present only the telling details.

(F) Now the story picks up again. In the heartbreaking details of Mrs. Rector's decline and death, we see the Hospice team constantly at work supporting her and her family—deeply involved with the feelings and struggles of every family member. We see a family counseled and comforted and able to remain whole in a tragic time. We sense that the constant monitoring of the Hospice team helped make Mrs. Rector's last weeks and days more comfortable and her end dignified and quiet.

Neither the Hospice team nor the Hospital is brought into the foreground of the story, except when it is natural for that to happen. This letter is the family's story. But the nurses are called by their first names and we see them almost as family members.

134

(G) These two paragraphs are truly poignant. I don't know whether or not the family preferred that the letter not be used, but this simple account of finding the letter and its contents is tremendously effective. One feels, too, that the letter should remain private.

(H) Could anyone write a more graceful, positive, affecting statement about a Hospice? This and following paragraphs do not need to go into detail about the number of clients served or man hours spent. The complete case for supporting Hospice has been made in the Rectors' story.

(I) The last sentence of this paragraph is one that might be the lead in many a letter. Here, it is the final new fact that closes the argument for a gift, brilliantly placed.

(J) This paragraph and those that follow down to the closing do just what they should, i.e., finish up quickly. At this point the reader is either persuaded or stopped reading long ago, so the letter-writer asks for the gift and closes quickly.

This letter is a masterpiece of direct mail fund-raising. It reminds us that fund-raising is a useful calling. I do think, though, that the gift range is too broad. I wish a version to donors had simply alluded to their last gifts and asked them to give at least that much or more if possible. This range is all right for prospects, but I'd like to see the "even" dropped in front of the $10—indeed, I think the paragraph might be expanded a bit, along these lines.

> "Because of the importance of this work I know that you will want to help if you can. People with many different incomes have chosen to help—some send gifts of $10, $15, $25 or more, others $50 or $100, some send gifts of $500, $1000 and even more.
>
> "Every gift is received with thanks and used to assure that the Hospice program will continue to provide loving care to all who need it."

The 40% response this letter reportedly received is so high I am sure the foundation mailed a note with each copy of the letter telling who suggested the other person get it. I've been involved in variations of this, and the credibility of the donor endorsement has a powerful effect on response.

Indeed, when you have a letter you feel is likely to be very strong, might you not enclose a note with it asking your donors to forward names and addresses of people who might also receive it? It would be important to ask for permission to use their names in forwarding the letters and to provide a well organized form to put the names and adresses on.

This letter clearly should be remailed by the Foundation. A strong letter can be mailed over and over and over to the same prospect lists with levels of success equal to or greater than the first time it was mailed. This point has been demonstrated in many large mailing programs, where the idea of a donor acquisition "control" package that produces a predictable level of response is well established. If ever I saw a letter that could be remailed successfully, it would be this one. One need only delete the holiday reference on page four.

About the Story

All direct response writers love telling stories. They know the printed word is a story medium and when you can get a fund-raising need expressed in the context of a story you will have a successful mailing. This letter makes the point undebatable.

But knowing stories outpull other fund-raising approaches is not enough. You still have to know what kinds of stories work best for your organization, and how they can be dug out.

There is no easy answer to this—it may basically come down to spending a great deal of time talking to program people about what's happening at their end, and listening for things that evoke your sympathy and concern.

STUDY UNIT

20

One of the best leads ever

(Sample: letter to prospects from Covenant House)

(A) (hour and date here)

Dear Friend:

(B) A lady should never get this dirty, she said.

(C) She stood there with a quiet, proud dignity. She was incomparably dirty—her face and hands smeared, her clothes torn and soiled. The lady was 11. **(D)**

My brothers are hungry, she said. The two little boys she hugged protectively were 8 and 9. They were three of the most beautiful children I'd ever seen.

Our parents beat us a lot, she said. We had to leave. The boys nodded mutely. We have to leave, one of them echoed. The children did not cry. I struggled to manage part of a smile. It didn't come off very well. The littlest kid looked back at me, with a quick, dubious grin. I gave him a surreptitious hug. I was all choked up.

I would like to take a shower, the lady said.

Fourteen years ago, I did not know that there were thousands of runaway, abused and abandoned children like these in this country.

(E) I learned the hard way.

One night, in the winter of 1969, six teenage runaways knocked on the door of my apartment were I was living to serve the poor of New York's Lower East Side. Their junkie pimp had burned them out of the abandoned tenement they called "home". They asked if they could sleep on my floor. I took them in. I didn't have the guts not to.

Word of mouth traveled fast. (It does among street kids). The next day four more came. And kids have been coming ever since. It was these kids—with no place else to go—homeless, hungry, lacking skills, jobs, resources—that compelled me to start Covenant House over fourteen years ago. Today our crisis centers help tens of thousands of kids from all over the country— and save them from a life of degradation and horror on the streets.

(F) Kids like the eleven-year-old lady and her very brave little brothers. They were easy to help: to place in a foster home where beautiful children are wanted and loved, and made more beautiful precisely because they are wanted and loved.

But sadly, not all the more than 15,000 kids who will come to Covenant House this year will be that lucky. These kids have very few options. Many of them will have fallen victim to the predators of the sex-for-sale and pornography "industry."

One of them put it to me very simply, and very directly: "Bruce, I've got two choices: I can go with a john (a customer) and do what he wants, or I can rip somebody off and go to jail. I'm afraid to go to jail, Bruce. I can't get a job . . . I've got no skills. I've got no place to live."

This child is 16. I do not know what I would have done if I were 16 and faced with that impossible choice.

They are good kids. You shouldn't think they're not good kids. Most of them are simply trying to survive. When you are on the street, and you are cold and hungry and scared and you have nothing to sell except yourself, you sell yourself.

(G) There was a time when I was forced to turn these kids away simply because there was no room. I can't do that anymore. I know only too well what the street holds in store for a kid all alone. That is why we run Covenant House, and that is why we keep it open 24 hours a day, seven days a week—to give these kids an alternative, an option that leads to life and not death.

(H) These kids come to us in need, from every kind of family background. Boys and girls. White, Black and Hispanic. Children—sometimes with children of their own. Innocent and streetwise. They are your kids and mine. Their number is increasing at a frightening rate.

We are here for them because of you. Almost all of the money that we need to help these kids comes from people like you.

(I) A lady should never get that dirty. And a good kid should not be allowed to fall victim to the terror of street life. As more good kids come to us, we need more help. We need yours. **(J)**

Won't you send whatever contribution you can in the enclosed envelope today?

(K) Thanks for my (no, our) kids.

Peace,

Signer

P.S. I'm enclosing a brochure that will tell you a little bit more about the thousands of kids who come to us each year. I hope you will read it, and give our kids whatever help you can. Thanks!

Suggested Study Procedure

1. Read the letter straight through at your normal reading pace. Ask yourself, "Good, bad, or somewhere in between?"

2. Re-read the letter slowly.

3. Use the CopyRater™ to evaluate the letter in detail. Add your score. Then note the most important strengths and weaknesses.

4. Compare your ratings with the author's at the back of the workbook.

5. Read the essay at the end of this Study Unit.

6. Write the suggested Exercise material.

7. Review all the work, then add the most important idea(s) to your own developing personal list of letter-writing guidelines.

Exercises

1. Short of rewriting the entire letter, please correct the biggest single weakness you find in this letter.

2. After the "wanted and loved" paragraph, write two paragraphs to show how Covenant House grew from the personal mission of one priest to being able to respond to 15,000 children (hint: thousands and thousands of people made this possible through giving, and they deserve a place in this letter, too. These paragraphs are to give the reader his or her sense of how he or she fits in.

Comments About This Letter

It is hard to re-read this letter today without experiencing sadness again about the human frailty that so beset Covenant House. Father Ritter's tragedy is also the tragedy of the great organization he founded and worked so hard to build. One can only hope both its idea and its work will continue.

This is a superb, and superbly written, fund-raising letter. It has surely been extremely successful. It's offered as a model of what can be achieved when a letter is intense, people-focused, and has a great story to tell.

(A) The insertion of the hour is good—it gives the reader a sense of how hard the letter-signer works and shows intensity of feeling.

(B) The lead is marvelous—it is in no sense a logical way to begin a letter, but it piques the curiosity in a way that mandates further reading. Just what a lead is supposed to accomplish!

(C) Super paragraph, but I want to point out especially the use of the word "incomparably," a brilliantly chosen adjective that is totally fresh in this context. All good writing depends on the imaginative use of words.

(D) "The lady was 11." The letter writer has great instincts—a lesser writer would have insisted on underlining this sentence just so no one would miss it. But it is far more telling when presented quietly. And briefly.

How much weaker—"The tiny little lady was just eleven years old"—would have been!

If you shout all the time (by which I mean underline and/or cap everything) you undermine the effectiveness of writing.

(E) If there is a key line in this letter, this is it, and again, the writer has the sense to make it a laconic paragraph all by itself.

(F) I love this paragraph! This is the one that (given the foregoing paragraph) brings tears to my eyes. There is an answer—these kids are not in a hopeless situation. But there are so many children, and so many wolves in the woods.

(G) The writer is saying, somebody has to stand *in loco parentis* to the children of the streets, who are the entire focus of the letter.

(H) The writer spends little space on how great and how many the centers of help are. He writes about kids.

(I) I'm trying to help, he says. Will you join me? Being a gifted writer, he says it in an enormously affecting way.

(J) Here is the simple statement of need for your help. I don't know if it would be helped by being expanded. The sincerity of the letter is such that this comment seems sufficient. Statistics would certainly not strengthen it.

(K) This paragraph is inspired. See how it shares the responsibility with you, if you'll accept it?

I normally suggest using gift range. But I understand the decision not to use one here. The principle being, I believe, to concentrate on enlisting the reader's sympathies and then to place suggested gifts on the reply slip.

This approach could draw a higher gift average gift size than a normal "$10, $15, $25 range" might.

I was involved in a couple of prospecting letters recently in which specific gift suggestions were left out and in both cases, an above normal percentage of response and an above average gift occurred.

This is exactly the kind of thing that's extremely important to test, because the conventional wisdom—and my basic approach—is always to say exactly what you want.

This letter is likely to be in use for a long time—in fact I don't know what could beat it—so what I would want to do with this specific letter if I were the Covenant House development director would be to "price test" different suggested giving levels to see what would draw the largest percentage of response.

Sometimes a descriptive brochure is helpful. This is one in that, if the letter has accomplished anything, it has inspired the reader to want to learn more about Covenant House. I like both using the P.S. to suggest people read the brochure and the repeated request for help.

A Question

It's clear this is a fine letter for a fine cause. But might it not pull still more strongly if copy were added to (a) increase the reader's role, (b) develop a specific ask, and (c) offer recognition, for example, "Will you join the Covenant House Associates?" I can't say that would definitely pull better, but I think it would be well worth testing.

And I'd test a specific suggested gift, on the premise it might induce more people to respond. Including a good strong reason to give now might also increase the letter's pull.

I'd want to try a computer-personalized version of this letter to some donor lists. There are opportunities for place personalizations related to the kids that could be quite potent,

"Where were she and her brothers from? They could have come from your own town, Scarsdale. Many of the children on these city streets came here from prosperous towns."

An appeal of this kind addressed personally could greatly increase a reader's feeling that "He really wants me to respond."

Test Offset, Extend Personalized

A company I worked for used to test prospect packages offset and if they looked promising, extend the mailings over larger list segments in personalized format. We usually saw the average gift go up without a drop in response percentage—up enough so the switch was economically justifiable.

A Final Thought

Many development directors working in less intense, more common situations might say, "Yes, that's a good letter, but look what they had to work with!" It's a fair comment.

If you are honest with readers, you can't paint a picture of your organization that is out of synch with reality. And few can compete with Covenant House for emotional content.

But all human service organizations have stories to tell. That's why these organizations came into being in the first place, because somebody needed help and somebody else needed to help. What happened when they came together—that's a good story right there.

Writers who want good response must find those stories and write them—people respond to helplessness, want, and to people striving to overcome great difficulties.

Such things are the stuff of the business we're in—it's a business of the heart.

CHAPTER

4

What Your Lead Paragraph Must Do for You

As Stephen King's novel *Firestarter* begins, a man and a little girl are running down a crowded street in New York City. Two men in identical gray suits are running after them. Although King doesn't say so explicitly, you feel certain the pursuers intend to kill both of them . . .

Who wouldn't follow that story a little further?

As a writer who has made millions of dollars through his instincts for what readers will find interesting, Stephen King knows it isn't nearly as hard to hold a reader's interest as it is to get his attention.

If you want to write an effective direct mail fund-raising letter, you have exactly the same problem to solve. You must find an interesting way to begin your letter. It is not enough, as many fund-raisers seem to believe, to state your case and watch the money roll in. You must get the reader's attention.

Why? Because readers look at the beginnings of letters to see whether it's worth taking time to read on. The lead paragraph in your letter is the stimulus that will either get a reader to read your letter or cause the reader to put it down.

Your lead won't by itself persuade the reader to give—but unless he decides to go on reading, you won't get the chance to make your case.

So it's sensible to think about your lead paragraph as having the sole purpose of getting the reader to go on. So as I said in Chapter Two, a lead that goes to reader self-interest, "We will be publishing the Honor Roll of Friends of the . . . soon and I knew you would wish us to include David Smith," is a natural attention-getter, as is, "I'm writing to offer you a leading role in the . . ." or simply, "Because you are one of our most valued contributors . . ."

The other basic type of lead that works well is one that does not so much "chime in" with reader self-interest as it distracts him from it. This is a news lead, and one that combines news and self-interest is almost bound to be strong—"Exciting news! A breakthrough in cancer treatment here gives you and your family a much better chance of . . ."

Because your own natural concerns are what's happening at your institution, it's difficult to write a reader-oriented lead—it's an unnatural act, something like a tennis backhand. But it's necessary!

My List of "Do's" and "Shoulds"

First, a lead must be written to one person. You may be mailing to a million people, but you are reaching them one at a time. You want to get a personal, conversational tone going from the very beginning. Nothing is deadlier than an "official" tone.

Second, a lead must draw attention to your letter, not to itself. Leads that are clever also tend to be response-killers.

Third, a lead must be interesting. Make the reader feel he is going to gain something by reading on.

Fourth, a lead should be brief. Unless it is extraordinarily interesting or important, readers will not stay with you through a long paragraph. Keep it inside five lines, tops.

Fifth, a lead must be written to the reader's likely self-interest. So, if possible, make your lead a reader benefit—make it news about something important to him.

Sixth, a lead must be believable. Take it on faith from the Con man that your reader is alert to a con—anything in a lead that doesn't ring true is grounds for discard.

Seventh, a lead must be natural. Nine times out of ten, the simplest, most natural lead is the best one. "I'm writing to you because . . ." is a good, safe, sensible lead. (And if "be sensible" conflicts with "be interesting," the latter should give way because readers respond best to letters that are clear and precise about what is wanted and why.)

Eighth, a lead should start a story, if possible. Eighty percent of the ten or so fund-raising letters I write each week are based on ''case history'' story-telling approaches—not because they're the most fun to write (although they are), but because they consistently outpull all other types of approaches. (It's not accidental that Stephen King is the best-selling author of all time!)

I always look for stories—a teenage boy fighting a lonely battle against leukemia, a counselor trying to reunite a family shattered by the birth of a severely handicapped child, a mother talking about the terrifying hours when her youngest daughter was rapidly sinking under Reye Syndrome. When you make it possible for people to feel the warmth of other lives, they respond.

Ninth, a lead should be as positive as possible. ''I have great news to share with you, food is getting through to the refugee camps in Ethiopia!'' People respond to both good and bad news, but they like good news a lot better than bad news! So in the long term, good news works better for you.

Tenth, a lead must begin the case for the gift. Maybe not directly—but it should certainly be beginning to point the reader toward the place you want him or her to go.

Eleventh, a lead must not be preachy. Terrible temptation, but people hate to be preached at and it's a guaranteed way to lose response.

The list of ''shoulds'' and ''ought to's'' and ''musts'' could go on and on, but maybe I can make it simpler. If you read the brief list that follows this just before you write your next fund-raising lead and again after you write it to see how it measures up, I think you'll have a good shot at a stronger-than-usual lead, which means higher than normal response.

> *1. BE INTERESTING AND POSITIVE*
> *2. BE BRIEF*
> *3. WRITE TO READER'S SELF-INTEREST*
> *4. MAKE THE LEAD BELIEVABLE*
> *5. MAKE THE LEAD NATURAL*
> *6. MAKE IT PERSONAL—ONE-TO-ONE*
> *7. USE A STORY IF POSSIBLE AND APPROPRIATE*
> *8. EDIT TO ELIMINATE ''WARM-UP''*

Editing Tips for Writing the Lead

Let me give you some tips based on experience. Start with the notion that every writer needs some ''warm-up'' time before the words are really flowing. That's why it's a good idea to look hard at the first few sentences of your letter and see if they are really needed or whether you were just getting cranked up. Readers respond well if they sense you are getting right to your point!

Also, please remember that all direct mail fund-raising is open book. Keep a notebook of good leads and study all the fund-raising mail you receive. Make notes on how you would strengthen each lead. It's good to go back through letters your organization has mailed in the past and rewrite the leads to make them simpler, warmer, more specific, more focused on the interests of the reader. Daily practice helps!

What Others Have Written

I'm not the only person working in these vineyards. Other people have thought hard and written well about what makes some letters pull like crazy and others die like ducks. The following ideas may be helpful to you:

D. Chase, The Copywriter's Guide: "A direct mail copywriter must learn to like people—all kinds of people. He must learn to understand them, to be amused by them, to sympathize with them. He must know what motivates them; what they want to be, do, and own. He must learn to think like the common man, to talk like him, and to write the way he talks."

John Yeck: "Put yourself in the other fellow's shoes. Be friendly."

Max Ross: "Phrase your first words several different ways and pick out the one best suited to your task. Keep trying to improve your lead."

William E. Sheppard's Fund-Raising Letter Collection: "When Cicero completed an oration, people used to say: "What a marvelous orator! What an excellent speech!" But when Demosthenes thundered his denunciation of Philip of Macedon, people leaped to their feet, shouting, "Let us march against Philip!" The same is true of fund-raising letters. One will cause readers to comment favorably because it is well-written. Another will capture attention . . . and get action . . . this is the kind of fund-raising letter we should write."

Jerry Huntsinger, Fund Raising Letters: "To get action, a letter must communicate on a deeply personal level. Tell the story of an individual . . . Establish geography, sex, age, etc; in other words, human characteristics that will form a sympathetic picture. Let your personality shine through . . . The only acceptable 'personality' is that of a warm, friendly,

148

compassionate person who strongly identifies with the donor and the people receiving help from the charity.''

Here are Fifty Leads (and Then Some)

- At 68, Ben Smith has just had a stroke. Now he is waiting for a doctor to tell him what his chance of rehabilitation is.

- I'm proud to announce that Doctors Smith and Dale of the Auburndale Medical Center staff have developed a new medical procedure that will save the lives of many newborn babies.

- If today is a normal day in America, 11,000 people will die of coronary disease before midnight.

- A busy father, looking for something to amuse his energetic young son, cut a map of the world out of a magazine and tore it in pieces. He asked his son to put the pieces back together . . .

- As a patient admitted by Dr. Johnson to this hospital earlier this year, you understand how important it is to maintain high-quality care.

- An event of great importance in your life has happened at the Auburndale Medical Center.

- Everyone feels lonely at times. But there are answers to loneliness.

- New York isn't the big unfriendly city Martha Chiang thought it was when she first came to America.

- After long effort, the Auburndale Medical Center has received state approval to purchase a CAT scanner. With your assistance, we can buy, install, and begin to operate a scanner by November.

- Lucy is the merest slip of a girl—two pounds and a bit—and no longer than this letter.

- In 19XX, when you were studying Engineering here at the University, thousands of alumni were quietly providing crucial financial support for the quality of your education.

- Last November my wife, 17-year-old son Tim, and I were on a Miami-bound plane. But it wasn't for fun.

- In our lifetimes we are tied by strong bonds of affection and loyalty to certain individuals and institutions—above all, to our families, churches, and schools. Each nurtures us and we do our best to sustain them in return.

- The two checks I've enclosed are real money—bank drafts, as a matter of fact. Therein hangs a tale!

- St. Valentine's Day was so exciting back in grade school! Remember spilling the contents of your brown paper bag of valentines on your desk, dying to find out how many you'd gotten—I do!

- Tim Smith (I'm giving him an alias here) lost an arm and a leg in the Mekong. That's a lot to lose! He could have come back to the states and packed his life in. But he didn't!

- If you'd been looking casually at the passengers waiting to board Flight 347 in busy Tampa-St. Pete Airport last week, you might not have noticed the worried young mother and her son.

- Of all the wonders of modern medicine, one procedure that would truly astound a time-traveling doctor from the past would have to be the transplantation of bone marrow tissue!

- If you were granted one wish this Christmas, what might it be? Good health? The sense that you are loved, that people care about you? That would be David's wish.

- The note had been written for him by someone else, perhaps a woman, but it was signed by a man in prison. I'm not good at this, he said, but I sure wish you'd help my three little girls if you can.

- When Ned trudged slowly up the long hill that rises from Route 8 to the Center, he was a beaten man—too weak to go on.

- You just need to look at Jason's smile to know what his mom and dad will count as their number one blessing this Thanksgiving!

- If Bradley Hill, the long-awaited child of an Auburndale family, had been born ONE MONTH earlier, he wouldn't be alive today!

- Lelia is blind, destitute, and elderly. Her one wish this Christmas is to see again—to watch the moon rise once more in the skies of her native India. You can make that wish come true.

• Summer may seem a long way off to a child, but believe me, it isn't when you're raising money to bring asthmatic children to a special camp—it's just around the corner!

• In May, 1983, Susan Smith was expecting a child. Her doctor noticed a decline in her white blood cell count. It continued to drop as he monitored her—

• This is a story about three kind people and one small white cat.

• We call them Children of the Silent Night, because the life of a deaf-blind child is quiet and dark. The ordinary tasks of living are made incredibly difficult by this double handicap.

• I feel as if I know you, though we've never met, and I feel as if we could be close friends.

• We are working against time in the effort to bring cancer under control—not clock-time, but people-time, because cancer claims the lives of about 1,000 Americans a day!

• One of four Americans now living will contract cancer. The odds are higher in some places than others—but they are much too high everywhere.

• Hyperthermia, the use of heat to shrink tumors, is a breakthrough technique that promises to take its place beside surgery, radiation, and chemotherapy as a major anti-cancer weapon.

• The Auburndale Medical Center is one of the major battle sites in the war on cancer. Researchers here are carrying out one of the most intense programs of basic and clinical research in the United States.

• Four-year-old Jenny is small for her age. That is a normal side effect of leukemia, the terrible disease that used to snuff out children's lives in months.

• As a parent, you invest countless hours of love and care in your children—an investment you make willingly because your children carry all your hopes and dreams. But some other children aren't so fortunate.

• A child brought up in a loving home is a seed in fertile soil.

- Some people define the quality of a town not by the size of the houses or the newness of the cars but by how the grownups look out for the children.

- Auburndale Boys' Village is celebrating its 25th birthday this spring. It seems a long time . . . and yet perhaps you or a loved one were defending America just a year or two before our first boys moved into the old farmhouse. Not so long ago, really . . .

- How big is the Thanksgiving Table at your house. Ours is thousands of miles long!

- As a child I learned the story of a traveler who stopped to help an injured man on a dusty road.

- I have a boy's future sitting right here on the desk in front of me. It doesn't look like much, just a manila folder full of papers. But what I do with it will change his life.

- This letter is about ink—two kinds—red and black.

- In a country of 230,000,000 people, Sarah is just one quiet life—a fragile life, growing up fast in a world of harsh realities. In a high school class photo, you wouldn't notice her.

- For $19.95 you can buy a good can opener. And that's not all you can do with $19.95.

- Last January a four-year-old named Peter was bitten savagely by a dog. While he was being rushed here by helicopter, his body temperature dropped to 80 degrees. His heart stopped beating at one point.

- People always talk about the luck of the Irish, but some children in Ireland aren't lucky at all. They need your help.

- If you were to ask four-year-old Sherry Cross's mom what makes her happiest these days, the answer might surprise you.

- Charity Clark, age three, still loves her dog pals Muffin, Blackie, and Fluffy, even though they made her sick for a while.

- It's late at night in Children's Hospital. Most boys in D Ward are asleep, but one four-year-old is wakeful. Fretting, he turns over and over, twisting the bedclothes.

- Children's Hospital has a "million dollar baby" named Howie. We call him our million dollar baby because it took so many dollars and specialists and months of care to save him.

- Who among us wouldn't answer a child's cry for help? I don't think many adults would have the heart to turn their backs on a hurt boy or girl.

- The alarm bell is ringing in our 30-bassinet Intensive Care Nursery for critically ill new-borns. Infant MacVicker is experiencing respiratory failure.

- Gifts like the $000 you sent last January helped our Trauma Center avert a tragedy for an Arlington family in April, Mr. Smith. (See how personalization can work for you?)

- I can feel spring coming as I write this letter. All this afternoon I have been sitting by the bed of a young girl who was sick all winter. Now she is slowly recovering. She's gone to sleep.

- Every time you send a gift to the University of Auburndale, that gift is permanently recorded here in your name, Mr. Smith.

- Whatever happened to Three Mile Island?

- Tonight, when the air is quiet, if you value your life and health and the health of your family, listen for trains.

- Plants don't weep but people do, and if you could see the damage the Auburndale Botanical Gardens sustained in January it might bring a tear to your eye, Mr. Smith.

Well, I could go on and on. . . . I love leads. You should too!

CHAPTER

5

How to Select Appropriate Suggested Gifts for Prospects and for Donors

"Your gift of $10 swiftly becomes a pair of shoes, a sweater, a coat to keep the winter chill winds off the back of a small Indian child."

I dedicate this chapter to Andy Andrews, founder of American Fund Raising Services, who wrote the brilliant "ask" paragraph above and who insists that "How much?" is **the** question in direct mail fund-raising.

Andrews says the amount of money you ask a prospect to send you is far more important than anything else in your letter, more important than what you need, than who you are, than how well your letter is written.

I agree. I've noticed during the past 22 years of working at this that the more space in my letter I give to a discussion of the money, the better response is likely to be.

Now why is that? That's because money is what a fund-raising letter is about. I didn't think so at the start, though. In my first days as a fund-raising copywriter back in 1970, I would write my letter, then ask the AFRS consultant whose client I was writing for to fill in the gift amounts.

You can make fatal ''ask'' mistakes in so many ways. You can ask for too much, you can ask for too little, you can make a donor's gift seem too small to be useful in getting the job done . . .

Remember, your cause is not more important to the donor than his or her daily life. And the dispensation of money is an extremely important part of that life.

What's a Good "Ask"

Here are the basics of a good ask, as I see them.

First, you make a proposition that's hard to say no to, e.g., ''Won't you send a gift of (blank), knowing children's lives are at stake?''

And then you ask for an amount that's possible and reasonable for someone to say yes to. ''Won't you send a gift of $10, knowing children's lives are at stake?''

Always follow your sense of what would be reasonable in any given situation with a donor or prospect. And remember, that you are always working for the maximum percentage of response in direct mail, not for the largest possible gift from a few, but for reasonable gifts from many. That's the fundamental arithmetic of donor prospecting and donor renewal.

When I hear someone say, ''We didn't get many responses, but we did get a few really large gifts,'' I am about to hear a horror story, because what I am really hearing is a lot of people saying no quite decisively and probably permanently.

''How much'' is the question the donor is always asking. And there are right ways and wrong ways to say how much, as I suggested back in Chapter One. Fortunately, if we use our instincts, experiences and common sense to dictate what we ask for, we will probably find the right giving level fairly naturally.

Major Factors Governing Reasonability

One is the type of organization you work for. I keep samples of 18 types of fund-raising organizations: ranging from religious orders to colleges to hospitals, museums, humanitarian appeals, environmental, et cetera.

Each of these kinds of organizations elicit a range of feelings from prospects and donors. A religious appeal, for example, elicits a very strong feeling from a religious person, while a hospital elicits a much weaker feeling from someone who lives in its service area. The likely intensity of those feelings in any case should be part of the way you decide how much to ask for.

Let me give you an example. A religious organization can reasonably ask for sacrificial giving because at least one aspect of what many donors are doing is laying up treasures in heaven. The more giving, the more treasures, presumably.

But on the other hand, the local YMCA had really better stick to modest upgrade requests in its Annual Appeal to its members. Because the feelings connecting donor and institution are by no means as strong as in the former case.

You just want to think hard about how likely it is that there is a strong emotional connection between what you are doing and your donors. The stronger the natural bond, the bigger upgrades you can ask for!

Another variable is the type of people you are writing to. As far as I am concerned, the world is populated by only two types of people: prospects and donors. Let's talk about each in turn.

"Asks" for Prospects

In prospecting, you are aiming to get as many "yes" responses as possible, so that you can build your donor list as rapidly as possible. You should not be looking for net money from prospecting. And so the hard "no", easy "yes" mentioned above is a rule of asking you can take to the bank.

There are two basic prospecting "ask" techniques, with some variations.

One is the single gift:

"Will you say "Yes" to an Indian child who wants an education? A gift of just $10 equals one whole day of school!"

"Won't you give just $5, knowing children's lives are at stake?"

The other is gift ranging:

"Because of the urgency of bringing cancer under control, we have received contributions of $1,000 and more from many persons, and gifts of $15, $25, $50, $100 and more from thousands of others . . ."

"Many friends send $25 or even more. If that is more than your family budget can afford, a donation of $15, $10 or $5 buys a powerful amount of hope . . ."

"A gift of $10, $15, $25 or more is all we ask. The boy in the bed could so easily be your child or grandchild or a neighbor's boy. Precious to us—but life itself to a parent. Thank you!"

This is gift ranging, or presenting specific suggested gifts that exclude neither the person who is a possible big donor or the person who is a small donor. You offer something appropriate for everyone.

Here again, there is interplay between the type of organization you work for and what you ask for. The cancer appeal above regularly turned up a number of large gifts—not, I think, because of the organization, but because the people who sent them had had a powerful and probably negative experience with cancer and felt very strongly about it.

I suggest that in choosing a gift range for prospects you find out as much as you can about the economic status of the people on your list and consider carefully how your organization might connect to them. The gift range will come out of that.

Another prospecting gift range that has worked for me is something I call the stretch technique.

"This need is so important that if you can easily send $10, I hope you will stretch and send $20 or even $25—and if a gift of $25 is not too difficult, won't you think about sending $30 or even $40 or more?"

When I have used this it has pulled the average gift from prospects up without appearing to cut into the response percentage. That does not get you more new donors but it increases your prospecting net income wonderfully—and that means, or ought to be taken to mean, that you can mail to more prospects.

Another technique that works is dividing a big sum into reasonable bites.

"This remarkable life-saving instrument costs approximately $25,000. For this reason we are hoping you will consider a gift of one, two, three or more Shares of Life at $25 per share."

Still another technique—What are Other People Doing?

"If you would like to know what people are sending, as of today 39 people have sent $100 or more, 65 have sent $50 or more and 612 have sent $25 or less."

You can present a high-dollar premium. John Groman of Epsilon has said that the best predictor of a donor's long-term value is his or her first gift. People who come in above your median gift will give far more than the rest of the file does over time.

So any way that brings them in initially at the higher level, so you can see them, and tend to their needs properly when they become donors, is extremely beneficial to your program.

Direct mailman Bob Hohler has often used this technique successfully. I think particularly of an offer to potential Unitarian Universalist Service Committee donors, who were offered a fine book on El Salvador, "Witness to War" by Charley Clements, who was then working for

U.U.S.C. This book was offered for gifts at the $100 level, in a P.S., and drew forth many new major donors.

A good technique in prospecting is to tie the gift to a Challenge Grant: "As a new donor, the Challenge Grant will match your gift dollar for dollar."

Something else that has been extremely effective for me, where it applies, is the localization of impact of a gift, for instance, "Won't you invest in the fight against cancer here in Samplecity where it would directly benefit the Sample family? A gift of $25 or more will do a great deal, I can assure you!"

I also remember doing a prospecting letter for a hospital that served a dozen or more communities in which we were raising funds for the hospital's cardiac rehabilitation program. We gave the number of people from the prospect's home town who had been treated for heart problems at the hospital in the previous year! The letter was very productive.

Some mailers have succeeded by presenting odd amounts.

In the classic "Hot Dogs for Thanksgiving?" mailing, Morgan Memorial Goodwill Industries in Boston asked for $4.70, an odd amount, to help pay for a Thanksgiving dinner for its clients.

And out in Chicago Larry Kroh asked for $17.87 to pay for a certain percentage of a hospital bed for sick children at LeBonheur Children's Hospital. Again, the results were strong.

"Asks" for Donors

Your main two goals for donors should be to keep them actively involved and interested and to gently, steadily urge them upwards by offering suggested reasonable gift increases.

What you need to think about as you construct your "asks" for donors is that donors are constantly changing their giving status. As I count them, there are (at least) first-time donors, regular donors, high dollar donors, lapsing donors, lapsed donors, sub-$10 donors, monthly giving club donors. The degree to which you use the computer to ask each kind effectively, based on his or her recent giving performance, will be a big factor in your level of response.

It seems to me that for each of these kinds of donor there are logical things to ask for and logical ways to ask. I'm pretty sure it's illogical, for instance, to ask lapsing or lapsed donors for a larger gift than they sent last time. Or to ask a sub-$10 donor for an increase that's more than double what they gave last time. Or to ask a first-time donor to increase his or her gift immediately. Or to ask your major donors to make big increases in their gifts when what is really important to you is that each one of them keeps on giving. (In general, when it comes to major donors, I say the more they give, the softer you ask.)

When you think about what state of mind each kind of donor is likely to be in, based on his or her recent giving history, what is reasonable or unreasonable will be clear to you.

Renewing Donors

You can use a donor's last gift to increase the likelihood of renewal in several different ways. Here are two:

Renewal by Recognition

"We are most grateful for your last thoughtful gift of $500. We hope this year you will wish to remain among the Hospital's Benefactors in the Annual Report by sending a similar or even greater gift."

Renewal of Lapsed Donors

"Looking at the records I found that the hospital last received a gift of $000 from you in June, 1985. Won't you consider renewing your much-appreciated support this year, Mr. Smith?"

Low Dollar Donors

With the low-dollar donor I have found that if you propose an upgrade that is very small, you will get a lot more upgrading going. For example,

"Can you possibly add an extra gift of a dollar or two to your regular one this time?"

Inasmuch as files of low dollar donors are apt to be very large, this kind of upgrading can be very profitable.

Upgrading Donors

"In view of this urgent need, won't you increase your last generous gift of $15 to one of $20 or $25 or even more?"

Do this and you will get a typical upgrade of 15% or more. Plus almost zero downgrading, because the last gift functions as a giving floor. I also believe that you tend to increase your overall response percentage when you propose to everyone a modest, reasonable upgrade.

Upgrade tables are in fairly wide use these days. The computer looks back at the last gift (some fund-raisers prefer largest gift, but I think last gift is on the whole a better index to most, if not all, your donors' current giving capabilities), says "You gave $000 last time, won't you give $000 or $000 this time?"

But not quite that baldly. You do a great deal better when you make a good case for upgrading as well as simply asking for it.

Here are some kinds of things you can request upgraded gifts for: an upgrade to meet a specific need:

"We need 25 of these beds for mothers of sick children, but as soon as 25 people send $25 apiece, we can bring one new bed to the children's wards immediately. Think what being there will mean to a young mother who's desperately worried about her hospitalized infant!"

Upgrade to General Goal Increase

"Last year Carnegie Institute received over $32,000 in gifts to the Appeal Fund . . . a fine start! This year, the goal is $40,000, a goal that can be achieved with your help, especially if you will consider a modest increase of your last gift of $000 to one of $000 or perhaps even more—thank you!"

Upgrade to Club Status

"We deeply appreciated your gift of $000 last spring and are hoping that this year you'll join the Friends of Children with a gift of $25 or more."

Do You Need a Computer?

Not necessarily. Writing for a public radio station a few years ago, we did a "Dear Friend" letter to the donors, in which we said,

"Go to your checkbook and here's what we need you to do: (1) Look up the amount of your last gift; (2) Write a check for 15%–20% more if you possibly can; (3) Mail your gift with the enclosed reply slip today."

We also added a line to the reply slip: "Yes, I am increasing my gift this time." As I remember, over 20% of the donors increased their gifts.

Copy Techniques That Increase Response When Linked to "Ask"

I've always felt that response increases and gift sizes increase when you expend serious effort dramatizing and specifying your need, as in the following two examples:

The Fishing Trip

The following text is taken from page four of a fundraising letter mailed in Canada raising money for an MRI scanner. Look how the gift range is presented, in the next paragraph and in the P.S.

> "In view of the importance of this new facility to people of this region, and its equally great research importance to Canada and the world, we ask men and women who can do so to consider contributing extraordinary gifts of $500, $1,000 and more. Such gifts are needed to reach the $6,500,000 goal and will be honored appropriately."
>
> "If you can make such a gift in your own name or to honor someone else, but you wish additional information, I urge you to call (NAME) (TITLE), at (PHONE). She will be happy to help you."
>
> "Yours sincerely,
> Signer"

> "P.S. I hope that everyone who receives this appeal will choose not to stand aside from a task that so clearly benefits all. At the end of the campaign, when the goal of $6,500,000 has been reached, we will present the Hospital and Dr. Sakharov with a list of donors. People who give $1000 or more will be listed as Patrons, those who give more than $100 will be listed as Sponsors, and those who give under $100 will be listed as Donors. Whatever the size of your gift, whether it is $50, $25 or any other sum, St. Boniface will be grateful and Dr. Sakharov will be made aware of your generous act. Help us

honor a great man and save lives—your gift does both, permanently."

The Bigger Fishing Trip

A few years back we ran this ad in The Wall Street Journal:

"We're looking for a $1-million donor to build a new child care facility that will be named after the donor. Call John Boomer, Child-Saving Institute, Omaha, Nebraska (Collect Calls Accepted)

CSI got a lot of press, local and national, print and electronic. And calls from humorous friends of John's. Plus one call from a lawyer who had a client who was interested in doing it. And did it.

So there's the value of a suggested gift—even though that one might not have sounded reasonable, it turned out to be reasonable for somebody.

When You Don't Specify How Much

Sometimes, in the case of a real disaster or a compelling need, it may be better not to put in a gift amount. I'm thinking particularly of Ethiopia, or the Vendome Hotel Fire here in Boston a few years ago. The thing is that people want to help, they don't have to or want to be sold on helping. If you leave it to them to decide how much, you may well get more than what you would have suggested. I don't say these situations come up all the time, but when they do, one should be alert for them.

Knowing Your Donor or Prospect

The Reverend A. R. Goodwin of Williamsburg, Virginia knew his prospect very well indeed. He got John D. Rockefeller, Jr. interested in restoring Williamsburg. Dr. Goodwin spent a great deal of time with Mr. Rockefeller in Williamsburg. But he never asked him for money, either specifically or in general. Instead, he allowed Rockefeller to be seized by the idea of the great restoration. He acted accordingly. Mr. Rockefeller made just one request—that was that while he lived, no one else would ever be asked for money for the project. And no one ever was.

CHAPTER
6
Personalization to Increase Response

In the Beginning . . .

I arrived in direct mail fund-raising in the late winter of 1970. I was a freelance writer with a commercial background picking up a letter assignment from the creative director at a direct mail company. The assignment was to raise money for a local hospital—and it was hard to believe what I was hearing.

"Let me get this straight," I said. "You mean when I write the copy for this letter, I leave a blank where a person's name should be and the computer fills it in? And the computer can also put the name of the person's home town in? And the amount of his last gift in?"

"That's it."

I didn't need to see statistics, I knew the letter was going to work like crazy. And it did—well enough to get me a job in direct mail fund-raising, well enough to build a wing on the hospital, well enough to bring me here, eighteen years later, to write you now about the power of personalization.

All because personalization worked amazingly well back then. And still does.

The hitch is that it needs to be applied intelligently—and sometimes a little imagination helps, too.

So, in this chapter I'm going to attempt to tell you what I've learned during the last 18 years about the intelligent use of personalization.

I'll pepper the text liberally with examples and provide full-scale letter samples that represent good personalizing at the end of the chapter.

What we are really talking about here are computer-based ways to increase the annual, quarterly, or month-by-month income of your organization. Not the big, occasional gifts—the small, regular ones that hold everything together.

But First . . . the Basic Arithmetic of Donor Base Growth

Good development officers make game plans in which the number of active donors is increasing as fast as possible and the income from each donor is increasing as fast as possible.

This means you must build in enough donor acquisition mail to replace the inevitable annual losses in your donor file (which run in most cases at least 20% a year no matter how hard the agency works to renew everyone).

In order to do enough donor acquisition mail, your mailings to prospects must be interesting and persuasive enough to come reasonably close to breaking even.

If they don't, a higher-up in your organization is only too likely to say, "This is costing too much, let's mail only to donors for a year or two."

This idea, which I've seen put in place more than once (and have argued against!), leads to a serious decline in income, due to the natural attrition rate mentioned above.

The goal of approximately breaking even is a reasonable one. What matters most in prospecting is the number of new donors you acquire, not the amount of money they send.

If your prospect mailing is at or near breakeven, you will go well into the profit column the first time that you renew the new donors. Why? Because each new donor is at least 50% likely to give again—and where you had to mail to 100 prospects to find, say, 4 donors in the first place, you then only have to mail to 4 donors to get 2 responses.

Quite a drop in production cost!

And even more important for the long term, after the new donor makes that second gift, he or she is far more likely to renew thereafter and will probably be contributing to your organization for years and years.

So that's why getting the maximum number of new donors at an acceptable cost is THE stake in prospecting.

When you are mailing to donors, on the other hand, getting maximum net income is the main goal.

To achieve this, your letters must, like the prospecting letter, be interesting and persuasive enough to keep your donors' attention.

And they must make people feel closer to your organization after reading them.

Above all, they must make each donor feel valued and important and recognized for the individual he or she is.

If this suggests to you very strongly that something is needed that works a good deal better than the old "one draft fits all" offset letter sent to "Dear Friend"—you're right!

And this is where personalization comes in. But not quite yet, because before there is personalization, there must be—

The Computer

Here's a comment by a very astute president of a small religious college that depends almost entirely on direct mail contributions from all over the country:

> "I want a (computer) system that will give me easy, fast access to accurate, up-to-date data, that will permit us to communicate more often with our supporters, that will help us identify good prospects, cultivate them, and convert them."
>
> "I want to be a record user, not a record keeper."
>
> "I want a system that will help me produce more dollars for my institution."

A computer, running under any one of several current software systems (FundMaster™ is one I like), can do all the above and more.

A computer gives you a way to communicate personally with far more people than you can contact on your own.

A computer is dumb, but boy, can it concentrate! And it never forgets anything you tell it, except in a power failure or a disk crash (the latter of which wouldn't ever happen to you or me, because we back up all our data, right?)

Creating the Donor Base

You can use a computer, inside or outside your organization, to create a donor base—i.e. a permanent, detailed record for each one of your donors (and key prospects, if you wish).

In each donor record you will store all the information you have a specific use for.

The way to decide what data you want to keep for each donor is to make a list of the contacts you now have with donors, the contacts you'd like to have, and what specific information would make all your contacts as effective as possible.

The essential information is full name, salutation, full address, a special "matchcode" you can use to remove the donor's name from prospect lists and to eliminate duplications, a detailed giving history that goes back at least five years, a second address, if any, a record of volunteer activities and any other associations between the donor and your organization.

If you have a membership structure, you want to code membership levels and expiration dates.

If you are a hospital, you want to code in patient exit dates and main categories of treatment.

If you are an institution of higher learning, you want to code in class year, particular school, if part of a university, and whether spouse also went to your college. These would apply to graduate schools as well.

You want records of capital gifts, memorial gifts, pledges, special events attendance, or other forms of special giving.

You want cumulative totals of the donor's giving, and what specific appeals he or she has responded to.

You want to be able to reach specific parts of the donor base with specific messages—lapsed donors, say, or people who have asked for once-a-year appeals, or pledge donors who get pledge fulfillment forms monthly or quarterly, or major donor club members. Et cetera.

And you want the computer to print out reports of response percentages, average gift sizes, upgrading versus downgrading percentages, cost/income analyses and the like.

I've looked at the software for donor base record keeping offered by a number of companies. Most of it covers the above.

The significant differences are in how easily you can include or exclude segments from a given mailing, how easy it is to reach back to the donor's specific last gift or largest gift (cumulative giving totals are rarely useful, in my experience).

And, I would say, in how well the donor base software works with existing mailmerge programs.

One thing that makes little sense to me in a donor base softwear package is to include space for data you will probably never compile and are even less likely to use.

If you are choosing a software system, the provision of space for things you won't use is overkill—and one way or another, that space will cost you money.

Personalization Made Easy

From here on, I'll assume you have a computerized donor base and that your software gives you a way to do all or most of the personalizing techniques outlined herein.

Please do remember, as we plunge into the heady uses of data, that personalizing is just one of the capabilities a good computer donor base gives you—the computer is like the palm of the hand and personalization is one or two of the fingers. We'll come back to these other capabilities as we go along.

For now, though, a few examples of personalization:

"Dear Mr. Squires:"

"If you came home from a trip to discover that your home in Nahant had burned down . . ."

"We were so pleased to learn that your son, Andrea, recently celebrated his 27th birthday . . ."

"I looked up your giving record and found that since 1975 you have contributed an average of $500 a year."

"This means you are automatically a member in good standing of our Silver Centurion Club, Mr. Squires, with the following membership privileges . . ."

Four good personalizations—granted, I don't have all the kinks out of Number Two—"son, Andrea"—yet, but that's in here to illustrate something important: if you want to personalize to get results, know your data is correct, or personalize not.

I remember a personalization by street for a mailing on behalf of The New York Hospital a fw years ago:

> "You and other people living at 450 East 54th Street should know about the advance in life-saving equipment at . . ."

We learned that about 25% of the people we had mailed to had post office box addresses.

If you change the personalization above to ". . . living at P.O. Box 383 should know about . . ." you might deduce that our results weren't too hot! But even though there were a lot of pretty funny errors in the addressing, the results were excellent.

Rule one of personalization is: you must have reasonably accurate data if you want to get good results from its use.

How Personalization is Done

As I use the word "personalization" here, it means the insertion of a name, address, or other data uniquely pertinent to one reader in one copy of a mass-produced letter.

A computer is connected to a letter-printer set to print a particular letter over and over. Each time the printer hits points in the letter text that are to be personalized, it asks the computer, "What goes here for this donor?"

The computer looks at the data file and picks the next item to be printed—it might be a name, street, recent gift, or anything else in the donor's record. It sends the item to the printer, which prints it and continues on until it reaches the next point at which a "variable" is to be inserted.

From the 1960s on, when the first computer-driven letters were produced, that has been the method. The big changes today are in the methods of data storage, computer hardware and software costs, the availability and ease of use of data, analysis of data, segmentation of the data file, and improved printers, especially laser printers.

Until quite recently, a donor file needed to be in the thousands to make creating and maintaining a donor base and printing via the computer economical.

New technology has changed that. Micro and mini-computers now permit the development office to store and maintain small lists right on up to very large lists.

And new printing technologies have made it economically viable to print personalized mail for any size donor list.

170

Basic Personalizations

The most common and simple personalizations serve the goal of simulating personally-typed letters. These include, in particular, an inside name and address and a "Dear Mr. Squires" salutation.

Because they are mannerly—who would, for instance, address a total stranger as "Dear Friend"—Shell Alpert, a great copywriter on the commercial side, calls such personalizations as "Dear Mr. Smith" and "don't you think, Mr. Smith . . ." "decorous" personalizations. I love it!

Such personalizations do have an impact on response. This is because people want their existence as individuals acknowledged and respected—perhaps above all, by the institutions they support.

Addressing them by name is basic!

Copy Style When Personalizing

Before we go beyond the "decorous" personalizations to more ambitious use of computer-based data, let's look at the differences, if any, in style between a personalized letter and a "Dear Friend" letter.

The main difference—I've seen it over and over and copywriter Jerry Huntsinger has observed it and written about it as well—is that the personalized letter needs to be low-key, reasonable, believable, to get best results.

Copious underlinings, dramatic statements all by themselves in bold-face, the use of two colors in the text, and all the other devices by which writers get people to read typically long, non-personalized letters, have little visible impact on the response to computer letters.

I believe this is because in a computer-personalized letter we have gone one step closer to a personal letter. It is from one person, it is addressed by name to one person.

If it makes sense, if the case is well made, if the tone is one you can easily imagine to be natural to the writer, then it is likely to be effective.

Personalizing for Donors

How do you get maximum income from your donors? One thing you need to do is to maintain frequent, friendly, personal contacts with them, based on meticulous, readily accessed records of what they have given.

Golden Rule Number One

The more thoroughly you can convince a donor that you know what, when, and why he or she gave, the more likely he or she is to respond to your current appeal.

Last Gift Personalizations

I think at least one of the following paragraphs, or something close, should appear in every letter you send to a donor:

"Gifts like your last one of $15 built this organization, Mr. Squires. Without your generosity, the Home for Wayward Squirrels would be just a forlorn memory today!"

"We deeply appreciated your last gift of $15, Mr. Squires, and we're hoping you can send one just like it now!"

Use of the last gift reference has proven that it increases renewal rates. A very common objection to using it has been that an organization is not sure of the data and is afraid of exasperating its donors.

To this objection, I say, get sure of the data—you lose more donors by not appearing to know what they have done for you than by an occasional incorrect figure. To me, use of the last gift is fundamental and crucial.

Upgrade Personalizations

Here's how an upgrade personalization works. You give your Mail-merge software a table of reasonable suggested gift increases, based on what each donor last gave, thus:

"In view of this new need, I turn to you, Mr. Squires, one of Enmity International's strongest supporters, to ask if you could increase your last gift of $000 to one of $000, $000 or perhaps even more."

The key to success in upgrading is that the increase be reasonable: thus, a $10 donor is asked for $15 or $20, a $25 donor for $30 or $40, and so on.

The jumps can get higher as you move upward—it is not unreasonable to ask a $100 donor for a $150 or $200 contribution—but keep it in mind that it is more and more important to retain donors as the dollar value of their gifts goes higher. You do not want to offend your major donors—each one is a precious resource!

The question is often asked, how often can you ask for upgraded gifts? That depends on what the organization is—if the donor's relationship is very intense, as in religious giving, for example, I believe you can ask for more virtually every time you mail.

But if you are a hospital, college or other similar type of institution, I think a once-a-year upgrade request is probably sensible (I don't mean ask a donor just once a year, I mean ask for an upgrade once a year).

It is very important to link a good "reason why" to the upgrade—the better the reason, the more upgrading will go on in the donor file (and the higher the renewal percentage is likely to go, by the way).

There are many upgrade variations—despite my recent dictum about always mentioning a donor's last gift, I've had good results with letters in which I did not mention the last gift specifically, only saying "I know either of these gifts represents an increase over your last one . . ."

It can be very effective in a letter to home in on a single upgrade gift, and to repeat it several times in the letter body, also in the P.S.

An extremely strong upgrading personalization I tested was asking donors of less than $25 to join a specific giving club, with special recognition, at $25.

"I am hoping that you will not only repeat your last gift this year but will increase it to $25 or more so you can join the Children's Circle of Friends and receive our newsletter and a beautiful poster."

This form of upgrading drew just as many responses as a more modest upgrade did—which made this a huge winner.

There are many upgrading techniques, for example:

> "I worked it out that if you could send just $000 that would be just a 10% increase over the $000 you sent last year, and that would mean that the Society could stay ahead of inflation this year!"

As you create donor personalizations, concentrate on two things: getting renewal, which means maximum focus on the importance of the donor throughout your letter; and getting an upgraded renewal, which means using a good deal of space and effort on the "ask" portion of your letter.

Personalizing for Prospects

To keep this section from reaching book-length, we won't start from ground zero on this subject. I'll assume you know something about donor prospect lists, i.e., why you need them, what they are, where to find them, how to choose lists that have a reasonable chance of success, how to know when you have had a successful prospect mailing, et cetera.

The further assumptions I will make are that (a) you have found a reasonably likely-looking list of prospects and (b) the names and addresses on the list are available on a computer disk or magnetic tape so that you can personalize your mail. (Most lists are available on computer media today, so that's a safe assumption.)

The way is now clear to send a personalized letter to a prospect if you want to.

The first question is, do you want to? This is not always an easy decision, because such a letter will cost you more to produce than a letter that is printed offset, but it will also be highly likely to deliver a higher rate of response and normally a higher average gift, too.

The decision you must make is whether the increased cost of a computer letter will be offset by the increased response and larger gifts.

Andy Andrews of American Fund Raising Services, maestro of personalization, offers the most sensible approach to this problem: he argues that you should mail a prospect package in an offset format in test quantities to see what its pulling power was; if it looks good you then mail the "extension" or "rollout" (a second, usually larger, portion of the list) in a computer-personalized format, because you know the extra cost will be covered by extra response (which means that you build your donor file faster, the main object of prospecting).

The simplest version of the Andrews rule: test offset, extend personalized. This way you minimize risk and maximize your chances of success, which is the right way to approach mail fund-raising.

But for now let's just say you have determined that personalizing your prospect package will be cost-effective. The question now is, how do you personalize it effectively?

You should start work on any prospect letter by assuming that your prospect knows little or nothing about your organization and is not the least bit interested in it.

The number one use of personalization in prospecting, therefore, is to GET the prospect interested. Remember that it is much easier to keep a reader interested than it is to get a reader interested in the first place. Enter personalization!

Personalizing Lead Paragraphs

Where do you put the personalization designed to get the reader interested? At the beginning, of course.

Put your key personalization in the lead paragraph, because if you don't arouse the prospect's interest there, your chances of success are over.

Here are some examples of personalizations designed to get prospects interested (I'll count the variables used in each example):

> "You and the rest of the Sample family should be aware that the Auburndale Hospital has started two cardiac rescue programs specifically designed to save the lives of Auburndale residents if heart attacks strike." (two)

> "If someone on Lake Avenue had a heart attack, it would take the trained paramedics of our new emergency unit just minutes to reach the scene and begin life-saving procedures." (one)

These personalizations use only name and address information. Now let's add information that your institution would have available—none of the following would be hard for today's MailMerge programs to add to your letters. See how they start to tie the institution and the reader's interest together?

> "If you join the Museum of Fine Arts, you'll be joining people throughout this area who share an appreciation of great works of art—and many of your neighbors because currently 325 of our members come from Auburndale." (two)

> "Heart attacks are even more common than most people realize. 437 Auburndale residents were treated here at Auburndale Hospital for coronary problems in 1988 alone." (two)

> "If a medical emergency should strike the Squires family, it's important to know you are just XX miles from Auburndale Hospital, one of the best community hospitals in the nation." (two)

The paragraphs above could go to just about anyone in the vicinity of your institution. They depend on information that's on the list and data about your services. Now let's personalize a lead paragraph as you might if you are mailing to a rented list of donors to causes like your own:

> "I know that no young member of the Squires family would ever be treated in the way that young Lucy was." (one)

"Mr. Squires, I've been told that you have a long history of responding generously to the needs of children who are in trouble and need help." (one)

"I understand you see it as a duty to do the Lord's work here on earth, Mr. Squires." (one)

"The list I found your name on suggests that you have an active and passionate interest in protecting the environment. I feel sure that your interest is not confined to what happens in your own state of Massachusetts—that it is much more far-ranging than that." (one)

Many institutions have lists of prospects with even more clear-cut ties. You might be a hospital mailing to former patients or a college mailing to alumni:

"As a patient admitted by Dr. Johnson to this hospital in recent months, you know how crucial it is for the hospital to be ready to respond to often acute medical needs." (one—a powerful one, by the way)

"When you were at the School of Engineering preparing to graduate in 1958, Mr. Squires, Auburndale alumni were carrying on a tradition of loyalty and generosity that was a long one even then. Now those alumni are gone—and we count on the men and women of the Class of 1958 to carry on the tradition." (four)

Personalizing P.S.'s

After thinking about how to personalize the lead paragraph, a second place I recommend personalization is the P.S.

Prospects and donors alike are said to look at P.S.'s when they are deciding whether to bother reading a letter.

That's logical because the P.S. stands apart from the letter body. And there is good evidence that P.S.'s have an impact on response. (For this reason, I recommend you always use a P.S., whether or not your letter is personalized.)

You use a P.S. to resell your basic proposition, to add a major fact, to offer a bonus, to establish a reason why it is important for the reader to respond now . . . and for anything else you can think of that is important.

I especially like to use a P.S. for points that would be distracting to the basic argument for a gift in the letter body, which is something I try to keep as direct, clear and fast-paced as possible.

In terms of personalizing P.S.'s, my hands-down favorite for both prospects and donors is an offer of recognition, thus:

> "P.S. If we receive your tax-deductible dona-
> tion before this month is out we will be pleased
> and honored to inscribe the name of Mr. John D.
> Sample on our 1988 Donor Wall of Fame."

(By the way, I learned to use the "Mr." above, so that when a client had gifts from "Mr. and Mrs," the computer would know to include them. A small point, but it might save you some grief!)

Don't undervalue the powerful attraction of recognition. People do want other people to know about their acts of generosity and you add substantially to response by letting them know that you do plan to recognize and honor their gifts.

> "P.S. We plan to display a Golden Log Book in
> our lobby and wish to enter the name of Mr.
> John D. Sample as a Dedication Sponsor in the
> Golden Log Book." (one)

> "P.S. This year a permanent memorial volume
> including the names of all donors will be added
> to the University's permanent archieves. We
> hope that the name of Mr. John D. Sample will
> appear in that volume."

Here's another example that will be familiar to attentive readers. It works well in a P.S. but better in a lead paragraph, I think:

> "P.S. Heart attacks are even more common
> than most people realize. 437 Auburndale resi-
> dents were treated here at Auburndale Hospital
> for coronary problems in 1988 alone." (two)

Other Prospect Personalizations

The three key parts of a letter are the lead, the "ask" paragraph in which you go for the money, and the P.S. If these are the most read parts of the letter, it follows that is where you place your personalizations.

A common bit of advice on computer letters is not to put in a person's name unless you have a good reason—don't just "stick it in" here and there in a way that violates common personal letter writing practice, e.g., "And that, John, is why you and the Sample family stand to benefit by membership in the Huguenot-Walloon Society this year. So, John, what do you think?"

Well, I agree, basically. Don't put names in for no reason. But in your "ask" paragraph, I think there is a very good, common sense reason to lead with a name.

I think we are visually drawn to our names in print, and so, when I have a paragraph that absolutely MUST be read by the prospect, I often write it like this:

> "Mr. Sample, we are really counting on your
> help, but whether you send a gift of $50, $75 or
> more as some friends do, or one of $10, $15, $20
> or more, please understand that your participa-
> tion is essential . . ."

In this case, the "Mr. Sample" acts as a flag to draw someone's eye to a key line or two, in this case the ones that ask for the money. A person's name is more interesting to him or to her than any other word. I don't know about you, but mine certainly is.

Segmentation

List segmentation is the basis for a different type of letter personalization. To me, it was the personalization breakthrough of the 70s—and I don't think its full potential has been realized yet.

List segmentation is employing the computer to keep track of each donor's behavior and then sorting donors of like behavior so that each person receives a letter that matches what is known about his or her current relationship to the organization.

In this kind of sorting the key factors are how recently the donor has given (recency), and how much he or she gave at that time (amount).

The factor of "recency" determines the likelihood of response to a current appeal—the more recently the donor gave, the more likely he or she is to give again.

(Yes, I know, that seems to fly in the face of common sense. What must be understood is that giving is not simply a drain on a donor's checkbook—if the nonprofit organization is doing its job right, its donors feel positive about giving, rather than negative. And when I feel positive about doing something, I tend to want to do it again soon.)

The factor of "amount" determines two things: one, how much you can spend on a renewal mailing package (using the very rough rule of thumb that the more you spend the more likely you are to renew); and two, how many renewal mailings you can afford to send in order to get a donor to renew.

I divide a donor base into the following segments: first-time donors; first-time major donors; recent multi-gift donors; recent major mutli-gift donors; lapsing donors; lapsing major donors; lapsed donors; lapsed major donors; low-end multi-gift donors; and quarterly or monthly pledge donors.

Though these segments do not change, the donors in them change all the time: donors turn from first-time donors into recent multi-gift donors, regular donors become major donors, and, alas, some donors of all kinds move into the lapsing and then the lapsed category.

Keeping these various groups in mind, you can create a basic appeal letter to donors and modify it to make certain each donor receives a version that conforms to the current relationship he or she has with your organization.

Thus, you might send an especially complimentary version of your basic letter to a major donor, a special "thank you" version to the first-time donor stressing the need for stewardship, a we've missed you version to the lapsed donor and so on.

The copy changes can be extensive, but often don't need to be. What is essential is that you center the letter around what you know about a donor who is new—one who is major—one who is apparently losing interest—one who is regular—and so on. If you make this relationship the core of your letter, you will receive a higher percentage of responses and upgrading than you would otherwise.

In addition to copy variations for the different segments of your donor base, you use segmentation to make production decisions that affect net income. This aspect of personalization is even more important than copy changes, so let's spend a little time on it.

If you arranged your donor segments in a rank order from most profitable to least profitable, you would place current major donors at the top of the list and lapsed low-dollar donors at the bottom.

With relative value in mind, it then makes sense to send both more packages and more elaborate packages to your major donors and to send progressively fewer and less costly packages to your lower dollar donors, with the fewest mailings of all going to your hard-core lapsed donors.

Last Stop

The man who gave me the freelance assignment in early 1970 asked if I'd like to come write for him full-time later that year.

"For sure, totally awesome!" I shouted into the phone. (I've always been a conversational trend-setter.)

At that time I had the somewhat solipsistic belief that the computer was a machine connected to my typewriter for the sole purpose of delivering my letters to millions of proto-contributors.

Since then, I have learned that there is a certain degree of mutuality—if the computer is tethered to me, I am also tethered to it.

During most of the 1970s, things electronic were slow to really take off. The computer letter continued to be extremely effective but wasn't the overnight *coup d'etat* that many had anticipated, partly because big hardware was needed to print it.

As far as I can tell, the offset letter continued to be the letter of choice for most organizations, mainly because it was cheap and familiar. But change was taking place. The process accelerated enormously in the late 1970s. Today, I think most development directors would agree that the computer is a better way where direct mail fund-raising is concerned. I hope so.

APPENDIX

1

Use and Abuse of Folders in Direct Mail Fund Raising

Let's start with a warning: during the past twenty-two years I have thrice seen a letter and a folder, in combination, tested against the same letter without the folder. In each case, the letter substantially outpulled the combination. And I've heard of other similar outcomes.

That makes the letter/no folder an especially big winner inasmuch as you get greater response and don't have the cost of doing the folder!

It's hard to make any firm rules in direct mail fund-raising, but I conclude from this data that a general descriptive folder (that's what was used in each of my three tests) does not increase the pulling power of a package. That's a very good reason NOT to mail one.

And if, as so often seems to happen, you have one lying around in quantity and you think it might be a good idea just to drop it into your next mailing—don't.

However . . .

For the past week or so I have avoided more productive work by organizing thousands of appeals I have been collecting for years.

One of my new file folders—actually, seven or eight—is labelled FOLDERS, SPECIAL PURPOSE. These are not general information flyers about the agencies making the appeals. Many of them you probably wouldn't even call folders. They are functional pieces that underscore and strengthen the message of the packages they appeared in.

I will list some of them here for you by type, because I certainly don't advise you to throw out the idea of doing folders altogether. Just make them work to serve your Copy Purpose, ie, raise money. Each time you write a letter, you might say to yourself, is there something I could add to this package that would add what they called "artistic verisimilitude" in the Mikado (". . . to an otherwise bald and unconvincing narrative," is the full quote. But of course, you're going to be truthful!)

Ideas for Special Purpose Enclosures

- A questionnaire or survey related to your theme.

- A full description and picture of the premium you are offering.

- A slip that provides a picture of your Book of Honor or Wall of Honor or whatever you use to recognize donor with.

- A folder that sells your membership benefits and levels. This is a must if you have real benefits.

- A reprint of a newspaper article directly related to your main point (Reader's Digest is by far your best source. Because of its famous level of credibility, if you have something good from RD, you can't miss!).

- A publisher's lift note, ie, "Read This Note Only if You Don't Plan to . . ." The lift note is usually folded in half and there is a brief additional letter inside, generally selling your main point. In my experience, sometimes these help the pull and sometimes they don't—but I've never seen them hurt the pull.

- A Prayer Request slip the donor can fill in.

- Simulated snapshots with handwritten messages in the back. We had a memorable one for the Franciscan Missionary Union in New York City. After their missioner in Peru and his assistant were pistol-whipped and their vital pickup truck was stolen by brigands, we asked donors to help the Father buy a new one. In a later mailing, after the job was done, we sent a photo of him and his assistant standing in front of the new one, with grins a mile wide. His assistant had his newly christened daughter in his arms!

• Personalized temporary membership cards. These are one of many kinds of "front-end" premiums, so named because they are given before the gift is sent. In one that I remember, we offered free admission to any of the properties maintained by the National Trust—in another, free admission to any Massachusetts Audubon property (get the pattern?).

• An official notice of some sort. I have a simulated Eviction Notice from the City of New York that was enclosed in a mailing to dramatize the problems of the poor. A teaser line on the outside envelope read, "Eviction Notice Enclosed." (!) The mailing raised holy hannah—and got a strong response!

• A Christmas Card or Chanukah card or card for some other holiday, appropriate to the time of the mailing. This is very clearly a response-lifter, especially to donors.

• A card on heavy stock that combined simulated handwritten and typeset messages with braille for "With Love." The mailer of this package said every time the brailled note was included, response jumped up. That was for The Lighthouse, I believe, but we also did it years ago for the American Foundation for the Blind.

• A poem (excruciatingly sentimental seems to work best) for a special occasion. In my youth as a fundraiser I wrote one of these for practically every mailing I sent out, and used them in many different packages for different agencies, and I almost always felt that they added response. Another front-end premium, I suppose.

• Drawings by children. Steve Thomas, a good Canadian friend of mine and a superb direct mailer, has been mailing a brilliant Easter Seal envelope covered with drawings by two girls, one of whom is an Easter Seal client. The drawings are so cheerful and bright—and response is excellent! These packages won a Canada-wide award for Steve and for Easter Seal.

• A "showmanship" enclosure such as pop-up art or a fancy scroll. A friend and I once lifted the style of "Amnesty Poster" that was originally for Jesse and Frank James (remember them?) in the 1880s and created an "Amnesty for Lapsed Donors" for a public broadcasting station in Boston.

Fun to do, but the response wasn't particularly memorable as being either good or bad.

• A list of equipment needs that bears out and expands the case being made in your letter.

• A folder that gives the technical specifications of a needed piece of equipment. In Manitoba four years ago we sent along the manufacturer's basic descriptive sheet for its MRI scanner, highly technical.

• A child's report card!

• A youngster's application for Fresh Air or other type of specialized camp.

• A postcard or postcards the donor or prospect is asked to mail, usually to politicians.

• A reprint of an ad that has run in local newspapers on the subject of the appeal. I think particularly of an ad that ran in the suburban papers here in Boston on the subject of a need for new surgical suites at an area hospital. We ran the ad three times, then reprinted it and used it as an enclosure. The campaign, which mailed to households in the hospital's service area, was very strong, and I am sure the ad had an impact.

• A special meal ticket for a poor person. A simple idea that has helped Goodwill Industries raise many many many many millions of dollars in Boston and around the country.

• A special prayer that is appropriate to the appeal.

• An invitation to attend a special new members' event in a package that is selling memberships.

• An invitation to visit a museum at a discount or free.

• Inexpensive decals—or in one current mailing, refrigerator magnets with the college motto on them.

• A copy of a newsletter from the agency, if it's interesting and oriented toward stories.

The Possibilities are Unlimited

Just make sure the folder helps you bring the money in.

APPENDIX

2

CopyRatings

Study Unit 1

1. (U) 2. (U) 3. (U) 4. (U) 5. (U) 6. (U) 7. (F) 8. (F) 9. (U) 10. (7) 11. (F) 12. (U) 13. (U) 14. (U) 15. (U,U,U,U,U,U) 16. (F)

TOTAL SCORE: 6

Study Unit 2

1. (U) 2. (U) 3. (F) 4. (F) 5. (U) 6. (P) 7. (U) 8. (U) 9. (U) 10. (U) 11. (U) 12. (U) 13. (VG) 14. (P) 15. (P,F,F,F,P,F) 16. (P)

TOTAL SCORE: 21

Study Unit 3

1. (F) 2. (F) 3. (G) 4. (F) 5. (F) 6. (P) 7. (U) 8. (F) 9. (U) 10. (U) 11. (U) 12. (U) 13. (U) 14. (VG) 15. (VG,G,G,G,G,G) 16. (G)

TOTAL SCORE: 50

Study Unit 4

1. (P) 2. (G) 3. (G) 4. (G) 5. (P) 6. (P) 7. (G) 8. (P) 9. (VG) 10. (F) 11. (P) 12. (U) 13. (U) 14. (G) 15. (G,P,F,P,U,U) 16. (G)

TOTAL SCORE: 45

Study Unit 5

1. (VG) 2. (E) 3. (VG) 4. (VG) 5. (VG) 6. (E) 7. (E) 8. (F) 9. (U) 10. (U) 11. (F) 12. (U) 13. (U) 14. (E) 15. (E,E,E,E,E,E) 16. (E)

TOTAL SCORE: 114

Study Unit 6

1. (F) 2. (F) 3. (G) 4. (VG) 5. (VG) 6. (G) 7. (U) 8. (P) 9. (VG) 10. (U) 11. (P) 12. (U) 13. (U) 14. (G) 15. (G,G,G,F,F,G) 16. (G)

TOTAL SCORE: 58

Study Unit 7

1. (F) 2. (P) 3. (F) 4. (P) 5. (P) 6. (U) 7. (U) 8. (F) 9. (U) 10. (U) 11. (G) 12. (U) 13. (E) 14. (G) 15. (F,F,G,F,G,G) 16. (G)

TOTAL SCORE: 47

Study Unit 8

1. (F) 2. (U) 3. (G) 4. (F) 5. (F) 6. (F) 7. (P) 8. (P) 9. (U) 10. (U) 11. (U) 12. (U) 13. (U) 14. (G) 15. (G,G,G,G,G,G) 16. (G)

TOTAL SCORE: 56

Study Unit 9

1. (F) 2. (G) 3. (VG) 4. (VG) 5. (VG) 6. (G) 7. (U) 8. (VG) 9. (U) 10. (G) 11. (VG) 12. (U) 13. (U) 14. (VG) 15. (G,G,G,G,G,G) 16. (VG)

TOTAL SCORE: 86

Study Unit 10

1. (F) 2. (VG) 3. (G) 4. (G) 5. (G) 6. (F) 7. (U) 8. (U) 9. (U) 10. (U) 11. (U) 12. (U) 13. (U) 14. (E) 15. (VG,F,G,F,F,VG) 16. (E)

TOTAL SCORE: 72 (thank you letter, many points n/a)

Study Unit 11

1. (VG) 2. (E) 3. (E) 4. (G) 5. (G) 6. (G) 7. (E) 8. (F) 9. (U) 10. (U) 11. (U) 12. (U) 13. (U) 14. (E) 15. (E,E,E,E,E,E) 16. (G)

TOTAL SCORE: 100

Study Unit 12

1. (G) 2. (E) 3. (E) 4. (E) 5. (E) 6. (E) 7. (E) 8. (E) 9. (U) 10. (U) 11. (U) 12. (U) 13. (E) 14. (E) 15. (E,E,E,E,E,E) 16. (E)

TOTAL SCORE: 132

Study Unit 13

1. (VG) 2. (E) 3. (G) 4. (F) 5. (VG) 6. (G) 7. (E) 8. (G) 9. (U) 10. (F) 11. (U) 12. (U) 13. (G) 14. (VG) 15. (E,E,E,E,E,F) 16. (F)

TOTAL SCORE: 96

Study Unit 14

1. (VG) 2. (E) 3. (E) 4. (E) 5. (E) 6. (G) 7. (U) 8. (E) 9. (G) 10. (E) 11. (VG) 12. (U) 13. (E) 14. (E) 15. (E,E,E,E,E,E,) 16. (E)

TOTAL SCORE: 150

Study Unit 15

1. (G) 2. (E) 3. (E) 4. (E) 5. (E) 6. (E) 7. (U) 8. (U) 9. (U) 10. (G) 11. (U) 12. (U) 13. (U) 14. (E) 15. (E,E,E,E,E,E) 16. (E)

TOTAL SCORE: 112

Study Unit 16

1. (E) 2. (E) 3. (G) 4. (G) 5. (P) 6. (F) 7. (E) 8. (F) 9. (U) 10. (U) 11. (G) 12. (U) 13. (G) 14. (E) 15. (E,E,E,E,E,E) 16. (E)

TOTAL SCORE: 109

Study Unit 17

1. (VG) 2. (E) 3. (E) 4. (VG) 5. (VG) 6. (G) 7. (E) 8. (G) 9. (E) 10. (U) 11. (U) 12. (U) 13. (E) 14. (E) 15. (E,E,E,E,E,E) 16. (E)

TOTAL SCORE: 130

Study Unit 18

1. (G) 2. (E) 3. (G) 4. (F) 5. (F) 6. (P) 7. (E) 8. (VG) 9. (U) 10. (U) 11. (G) 12. (G) 13. (E) 14. (E) 15. (E,E,E,E,E,E) 16. (E)

TOTAL SCORE: 115

Study Unit 19

1. (E) 2. (E) 3. (F) 4. (F) 5. (F) 6. (F) 7. (E) 8. (E) 9. (U) 10. (U) 11. (E) 12. (U) 13. (G) 14. (E) 15. (E,E,E,E,E,E) 16. (E)

TOTAL SCORE: 116

Study Unit 20

1. (E) 2. (E) 3. (E) 4. (F) 5. (F) 6. (F) 7. (E) 8. (F) 9. (U) 10. (U) 11. (U) 12. (U) 13. (VG) 14. (E) 15. (E,E,E,E,E,E) 16. (E)

TOTAL SCORE: 110

NOTE: The CopyRater™ is a *collection* of things to do and approaches to take that commonly increase response. But any letter written *just* to utilize every item on the list probably wouldn't do all that well. No letter is a collection of techniques. I believe that it logically follows that a high score on the CopyRater™ alone is not a guarantee of tremendous success in the mail (the opposite is what is both true and useful to know—if your letter scores low on the CopyRater™, below 50, say, it is almost certain to do badly).

If you look at the letters in Study Unit Nineteen and Twenty, in particular, both really exceptional letters, the scores are clearly lower than the real pulling power of the letters. But even here the CopyRater™ is useful—it is reasonable to say about about both letters that if more attention had been given to the readers, and more specific "asks" had been set, they would probably have pulled even better. Thus the CopyRater™ can help you in the editorial review stage by reminding you of things you may have left out.

APPENDIX

3

The CopyRater™

THE COPYRATER
How to Evaluate a Lette

Use this COPYRATER to rate the major factors governing response to a letter. Add points this wa
0 for Unsatisfactory, 1 for Poor, 2 for Fair, 4 for Good, 6 for Very Good, 8 for Excellent.

	0	1	2	4	6	8
1. Emotional Intensity Intense, swift-reading.	☐	☐	☐	☐	☐	☐
2. Lead Get reader involved, state problem, give news.	☐	☐	☐	☐	☐	☐
3. Problem Immediate, specific, people-centered.	☐	☐	☐	☐	☐	☐
4. Solving Problem Solution direct, time-related, money-related.	☐	☐	☐	☐	☐	☐
5. Concentration on Reader's Role Show how reader solves problem. Show gift in use. List reader benefits.	☐	☐	☐	☐	☐	☐
6. Institutional Ego Grade by how little letter is about institution, how much about reader.	☐	☐	☐	☐	☐	☐
7. Storytelling Best letters often start with stories–all letters should have story elements.	☐	☐	☐	☐	☐	☐
8. "Ask" Specific, detailed, uses more than one paragraph.	☐	☐	☐	☐	☐	☐
9. Recognition Recognition offered donor.	☐	☐	☐	☐	☐	☐

Add points from each column.
Enter total in last box.
Carry total forward to next page.

☐ + ☐ + ☐ + ☐ + ☐ + ☐ = ☐

THE COPYRATER	0	1	2	4	6	8
0. Reason to Give Now Strong reason.	☐	☐	☐	☐	☐	☐
1. Suggested Gift Money specific, clear, appropriate to reader–i.e., low for prospects, higher for donors.	☐	☐	☐	☐	☐	☐
2. Upgrading If to prior donor, should suggest reasonable, manageable upgrade	☐	☐	☐	☐	☐	☐
3. P.S. Restate case urgently, include deadline.	☐	☐	☐	☐	☐	☐
4. Extraneous Material No ideas except those needed in case for gift.	☐	☐	☐	☐	☐	☐
5. Readability						
Friendly, Personal	☐	☐	☐	☐	☐	☐
Reads quickly	☐	☐	☐	☐	☐	☐
Down-to-earth words	☐	☐	☐	☐	☐	☐
Easy, brief sentences	☐	☐	☐	☐	☐	☐
Brief paragraphs	☐	☐	☐	☐	☐	☐
Good paragraph flow	☐	☐	☐	☐	☐	☐
6. Appropriate Copy for Mailing List Based on what is known about mailing list.	☐	☐	☐	☐	☐	☐

Add points from each column. Enter total in last box. ☐ + ☐ + ☐ + ☐ + ☐ + ☐ = ☐

Subtotal from other side. .... + ☐

Add totals of each page for total score. (168 possible) .... = ☐

Your score of 100 or more for a letter suggests that many effective techniques are being utilized and is therefore a strong predictor that the letter will draw a good response, with the important qualification that is going to an appropriate mailing list! A score of 75 or less means that majhojr problems must be addressed nd corrected before the letter is mailed.)

INDEX

Writer, consultant and teacher Conrad Squires has helped hundreds of nonprofit agencies raise money by mail since he began working as a direct response fund-raiser in 1970. He is president of the National Copy Clinic, Inc., and publishes the newsletter, **The Direct Response Donor.** Inquiries concerning newsletter subscriptions or Con's creative or teaching services should be addressed to the National Copy Clinic, Inc., 22 Lake Avenue, Auburndale, MA. 02166, or call 1-800-845-1608.